EAST
WEST
TRADE

AND
UNITED STATES
POLICY

by MOSE L. HARVEY

with a foreword by:
AMBASSADOR ROBERT D. MURPHY

NATIONAL ASSOCIATION OF MANUFACTURERS

277 Park Avenue ■ New York, N. Y. 10017

benefits produced for the Soviet Union. And the same holds for the accelerating trade of Western Europe and Japan with the communists. The United States, rather than being lured by these apparent bonanzas into breaking with its long-established policies of restricting trade, should look upon these new developments as added reason for standing firm.

A growing body of opinion, however, appears in favor of liberalizing existing U. S. practices. The gist of the catechistic-type argument underlying this point of view is as follows:

Conditions have altered drastically since the restrictive system was established; it is now beyond Western capacity to affect substantially communist (Soviet) military strength or economic development; in any event, Western Europe and Japan freely trade in goods other than items of direct military importance, and the communists can procure virtually anything they need from those sources; the only effect of continued U. S. restrictions is, therefore, to deny American business a fair share of a lucrative market; further, the expansion of U. S. trade with the European communists would serve useful ends in that it would open the way for increased contacts, make for a relaxation of tensions and lay foundations for better political relations, reduce the dependence of communist states on each other, encourage greater communist concentration on the export industries, reduce communist self-sufficiency, help U. S. business and labor, and ease the U. S. balance of payments problem.

An Authoritative Voice for a New Policy

Climaxing the trend toward a change in the U. S. stance, a Special Committee appointed by the President has laid a quasi-official basis for adoption of a new approach. This Committee—popularly known as the "Miller Committee" in honor of its Chairman, J. Irvin Miller of the Cummins Engine Company—was created on February 16, 1965. Its task:

> "To explore all aspects of expanding peaceful trade in support of the President's policy of widening constructive relations with the countries of Eastern Europe and the USSR."

In its *Report* of April 29, 1965, the Committee's key recommendation was that the United States:

> "Use trade negotiations with individual communist countries more actively, aggressively, and confidently in the pursuit of our national welfare and world peace."

The Committee, while making this and other recommendations,

4

on Foreign Relations. On March 13, 1964, the Committee began hearings aimed at a re-examination of the premises underlying current U. S. policies. The central issue as seen by the Committee was spelled out by the acting chairman in these terms:

> "One vital question is whether the basic U. S. trade policies toward the Communist Bloc formulated around 1950 are now fully valid a decade and a half later. If they are, they should be restated and clarified, and greater efforts should be made to persuade Western Europe of their merits. On the other hand, if those policies are geared to conditions which no longer exist, serve only to penalize American businessmen, disrupt our relations with our allies, and fail to promote our basic foreign policy objectives, they must be brought up to date."

The initiative taken by the Committee broke with the tradition of a jealous Congressional watchfulness over the sanctity of the restrictive system, and freed administrative officials of the inhibiting restraints that this watchfulness had produced. It also gave courage to speak out to those business elements most directly affected by restrictions, those who hitherto had stood under the shadow of a charge that they would put self-interest above national interest, that they would barter the security of their country for a mess of pottage for themselves.

The Committee itself has elicited and publicized the views of key Administration figures, selected representatives of the business and financial communities, and various academic experts. News and opinion journals, newspaper columnists and editorialists, and a wide variety of business, trade and professional organizations have picked up and extended the discussion.

A great and mounting volume of commentary has thus been built up around the question of whether U. S. trade policies toward the East should hew to the established line, depart from it entirely, or introduce important new variants. Hardly a facet of the over-all problem has failed to elicit thoughtful exploration from a variety of angles. And hardly a possible point of view has failed to get expression.

Pro and Con Positions

In the unfolding debate, strong voices still speak for continuation of existing practices. For many, the wheat deal and the flourishing trade of our allies with the communist countries have served to generate alarm rather than a desire for the United States to get in on a "good thing." That the Soviet Union was willing to buy U. S. wheat, and for gold, is seen by these as sure proof of the dependence of the USSR on western sources of supply. Whatever gain the U. S. may have derived from the sale of this wheat was, in their minds, small in comparison with the become consumer items, such as the sale of wheat exports are clearly justified and of real value to the United States. Secretary Rusk made the point that sales of U. S. wheat to the Soviet Union were of relatively marginal importance to them. If their economy is strengthened, then the position of the United States is strengthened even more. The USSR has apparently been forced to sell substantial portions of their extremely limited stocks of gold to pay for these imports. We have gained both by increased foreign exchange and diminished surpluses. We have scored another gain which, in the long run, may be of even more value in the world propaganda field. Most of the developing and emerging nations of the world are hungry. They search eagerly for the best methods of achieving economic development and higher living standards. An abundance of food is very important to them. When the strongest communist nation must purchase wheat from a nation that has enough both to spare and to share, a significant propaganda victory has been scored for our way of life. We should make as great a use of it as possible. For all of these reasons, the bargain we are making in selling wheat and similar agricultural commodities to the Soviet bloc strengthens our position far more than it does the position of the communists."

Even greater and more far reaching has been the impact of the mounting flow of goods from Western Europe and Japan to the communists. While U. S. trade with the USSR and other countries of Eastern Europe remains in the range of the tens of millions (less than a hundred million dollars a year exclusive of the specially arranged trade with Poland), that of the other advanced Western countries has mounted to the billions (between four and five billion dollars annually since 1960).

Other factors have also come to influence opinion. On the one hand is a sense of failure of U. S. efforts to use trade denial to retard the growth of the military potential of the communist countries; on the other is the feeling that the United States is obligated, both in terms of self-interest and in terms of the world, to explore every possibility of new kinds of relationships between itself and the communist powers, particularly the USSR. The thinking is that in its trade policy the United States has a means to make a gesture toward the USSR that will, without cost to the United States, show its willingness to meet the Soviet leadership half-way in any movement toward a genuine rapprochement. Moreover, through an expansion of trade with the U. S., it is felt that the Soviet Union will come to have an increasingly important stake in holding down tensions, and that trade contacts will necessarily serve to break down the barriers that have so long divided the communist and noncommunist worlds.

Role of the Foreign Relations Committee of the U. S. Senate

A focal point of the public inquiry has been the Senate Committee

PART 1

INTRODUCTION: BASIC CONSIDERATIONS

What is the United States to do about its long-standing policy of restricting trade with the communist countries? The question remains high on the agenda of national policy problems. The Congress on June 30, 1965 extended the Exports Control Act of 1949, as amended, for a four-year period ending June 30, 1969. But it did so without debate, with the evident tacit understanding of both the Administration and legislative leaders that this was a holding action taken in response to the worsening of the Vietnamese crisis, and that a new look will be taken at the whole matter some months hence when and as the international climate improves.

When that time arrives, the Congress can be expected to weigh the results of a searching public inquiry into the efficacy of our restrictive policies.

Chapter One

THE BACKGROUND

Why the Review?

This promised inquiry, which would follow years of a near-sacrosanct status for those policies, was mainly sparked by two circumstances: first, the sale for cash of approximately 1,700,000 metric tons of U.S. wheat to the Soviet Union in January and February 1964, and second, a spectacular increase over the past several years in the volume of exports by other industrialized countries of the West to the communist countries of Eastern Europe.

These two events served to whet appetites and generate high expectations in important elements in the United States. The wheat deal was seen as a major boon for this country, and only marginally advantageous, if not downright disadvantageous, for the USSR. Secretary of Agriculture Orville Freeman's statement in March, 1964 before the Senate Committee on Foreign Relations, illustrates this attitude:

"For consumer goods—particularly agricultural commodities that will

1

ix

TABLE OF CONTENTS

v

officials of the National Association of Manufacturers who are responsible for the task being undertaken, and particularly President W. P. Gullander, who has been most cooperative. I am deeply grateful for their patience, as well as for the scrupulous manner in which they refrained from trying to influence in any way the content or the views presented.

Ambassador Robert Murphy, Chairman of the International Economic Affairs Committee of the NAM, has contributed of his wisdom in penetrating discussions of the various problems to be dealt with and the questions we need to ask about them.

Mr. Jaime Suchlicki, a graduate student at the University of Miami who is now continuing his studies at Texas Christian University, worked tirelessly as a helpful researcher and an indispensable Man Friday. My son, Dodd Lofley Harvey, gave invaluable assistance in the statistical analysis department, and made valiant, if mostly vain, efforts to secure appropriate attention to and respect for the intellectual tools and techniques of the professional economist.

I owe a special debt to Mr. Edward R. Fried, a long-time friend and close associate in the field of analysis and planning in the Department of State, who served as Executive Secretary to the Special Presidential Committee on U. S. Trade Relations with the East European countries and the Soviet Union. Mr. Fried has no responsibility whatsoever for either the content or views of the study. He might well differ strongly with much if not most of what is said. My indebtedness to him arises from the sharing of work, including a frequent clash of opinion, on the same subject while we were both members of the Policy Planning Council of the Department of State.

Finally, there is the great debt to my wife, Ruth Vaughn Harvey, without whose unfailing solicitude the whole business would never have gotten off the ground.

M. L. H.

Center for Advanced International Studies
The University of Miami
Coral Gables, Florida
August, 1965

A PREFATORY NOTE

An associate on reading the manuscript of this study remarked that it was not a monograph on East-West trade but a somewhat disjointed dissertation on trade and the cold war. If the study has any value, it derives from just this feature. For the problem of our East-West trade policy cannot be separated from the gamut of problems forced upon us by the cold war, or from the gamut of policies we are following in pursuit of our objectives in that contest.

Some seem to think otherwise. They see the possibility of a trade relationship between the United States and the communist countries of Eastern Europe, particularly the USSR, on an entirely different plane and operating under an entirely different set of rules than mark our other relationships.

Some even see trade between the United States and the communists as a means of bridging the hostility gap and conflict between our two systems. As all would surely agree, this would be fine if it would work. The difficulty is that our adversaries, first and foremost the USSR, treat foreign trade as a weapon, and an important weapon at that, in the continuing struggle they wage against us. Foreign trade policy for the communists is an element in cold war policy. This is the most elementary, and the most important, consideration to keep in mind as we look at our own trade policies.

I have not attempted in the study to examine all aspects of the East-West trade problem. A reading will leave many obvious questions unanswered. Little in the way of historical background is given; statistical data have been held to a minimum; and technical details of how trade is conducted between ourselves and the communists, on both sides, have been passed over. The reason is, as the title indicates, I have sought to concentrate on policy issues. The aim is analysis, for whatever it is worth, not a descriptive factual accounting.

Despite the relative brevity of the text, the debt I owe to others is far too extensive to be acknowledged in detail. I would be remiss, however, if I did not note the thoughtful counsel and assistance of the

Dr. Harvey has been the recipient of post-doctoral fellowships and research grants for work in the Soviet field, including work in the Soviet Union and with organizations such as the Council on Foreign Relations. He taught and directed research on Soviet and communist affairs at Emory University, Johns Hopkins, the School of Advanced International Studies in Washington and the National War College.

During World War II, Dr. Harvey served as principal officer in the War Production Board on Soviet supply matters. He worked as a consultant to the Department of State in connection with the establishment of a United States psychological program regarding the Soviet Union and Eastern Europe. His assignments in the Foreign Service included the post of Deputy Chief of Mission at Helsinki, Finland, and Deputy United States Representative to the International Atomic Energy Agency in Vienna, Austria.

Dr. Harvey's present paper merits attentive consideration.

ROBERT MURPHY
Chairman
Corning Glass International (SA)
and
Chairman, NAM International Economic Affairs Committee

FOREWORD

In September of 1964, the National Association of Manufacturers, because of its deep interest in international economic affairs, commissioned Dr. Mose Harvey to prepare this monograph on "East-West Trade and United States Policy." NAM was motivated in this undertaking by a desire to illuminate a very controversial subject.

I am confident that the reader will feel, as I do, that Dr. Harvey has handled his subject well; that he has amassed the critical facts about East-West trade that leaders of government and business must weigh carefully; and that he has drawn some compelling conclusions. It is clear, indeed, that this book merits the careful consideration not only of the American public but of the peoples and governments of allied countries and of the developing nations.

Dr. Harvey delineates his views as to why United States trade denial policy should continue as an integral part of a strategic national design developed over four successive administrations.

He suggests that in view of the significant changes which have taken place within the USSR over the past decade, there exists the possibility of the United States exerting influence by continuing to deny trade or through granting access to the United States market on a strictly conditioned and judiciously controlled basis. The present situation permits a trial of alternatives within the framework of long established United States strategic objectives.

Dr. Harvey is the Director of the University of Miami's Center For Advanced International Studies. Until recently, he was a Senior Member of the Policy Planning Council of the Department of State with special responsibility for policy matters relating to the USSR and the communist world generally. He has had extensive training and long experience as a career Foreign Service officer before taking up his present post at the University of Miami. His bachelor's and master's training at Emory University in Atlanta, Georgia, concentrated in the area of Russian history; his Ph.D. treatise for the University of California dealt with the Soviet economy and Russian economic history.

i

showed an acute awareness of the political complexities of trade with the communists and of a U. S. need for continuing safeguards. It emphasized that "political, and not commercial or economic considerations, should determine the formulation and execution of our trade policies." It rejected any thought of subsidizing the trade or of otherwise giving it "artificial encouragements." And it excluded trade "in items that could significantly enhance communist military capabilities." Subject to these cautions, however, it believed that with respect to the European communists:

> "The amount of trade that takes place should be left to U. S. business and the U. S. consumer to decide."

For in its view:

> "In terms of foreign policy considerations . . . trade with European communist nations can be as much in the national interest as any other trade."

Chapter Two

THE REQUIREMENT: TO PROMOTE THE NATIONAL INTEREST

What should be the attitude of the American people toward the findings and recommendations of this Committee? How are we to look on the whole matter of a possible reversal of a course which we have followed for a decade and a half? The temptation can be strong to let emotions determine the answers. On the one side is repugnance at the very thought of increasing trade with an avowed enemy; on the other is anger that allied nations, with as much at stake as we, engage freely and profitably in a trade we deny our own business community. But emotions, whichever way they pull, can be a poor guide to good policy.

Policy must be decided on a sounder basis than clichés and platitudes, or chagrin or envy, or some other such irrelevancy; it must be decided on the same basis as should govern in the case of any other foreign policy. Judgment should reflect an objective accounting of costs and benefits of one policy as against another, of the relative effectiveness of varied alternatives. There is a special need to avoid oversimplifying or by-passing complex issues. Often, lines are too sharply drawn; too much is taken for granted; too little attention is paid to limitations and to built-in consequences of certain lines of action; self-contradictory positions too glibly are taken and defended; doubtful assumptions are accepted as verities. We must recognize that the issues raised by the East-West problem are intertwined with other issues, that they must be viewed in perspective. We must accept that in the present world situation foreign trade cannot be looked upon as something of and by itself; it must be seen as part of a complex whole of interrelated and interacting factors and requirements.

The Political Factor in Foreign Trade

The one matter on which we must keep our attention concentrated is the national interest of the United States. The fundamental question we have to decide is what will best and most directly serve our basic security objectives.

Some would have it that except in time of war, foreign trade is a commercial and not a political matter; that the object of trade is the mutual economic benefit of the trading partners; that the national interest of each of the partners will automatically be furthered by its sharing in that mutual benefit; and that any interference in the flow of trade is apt to be as damaging to the instigator as to the target.

Much of this thinking is due to the concept that foreign trade is somehow a moral matter. And this marks both extremes in the argument over whether we should continue to limit or liberalize trade. The one group views the restrictive policy as a morally necessary consequence of an assumed innate immorality of trade with communists. The other group views unhampered trade, except in actual war, as a sort of moral requisite from the standpoint of both the right of the individual and the obligation of a democratic state—but evidently only a democratic state—to other states, or better to the international order.

As a matter of fact, foreign trade *as such* is no more a moral matter than domestic trade. Unless and until a special interest of the state is involved and is expressed in a law or regulation, foreign trade is strictly an economic matter. As an economic matter, it is "good" or "bad" only in terms of the economic results it achieves. When state interests are interjected through laws or regulations, then foreign trade in violation of these becomes illegal or even disloyal, and in this sense "immoral." But it is a political judgment, a given political policy, which makes it so. Conversely, nothing about foreign trade—any sort of foreign trade—makes it "wrong" for a state to regulate it in any way it sees fit.

In practice, of course, states invariably have an interest in foreign trade and invariably subject it to regulations in accord with that interest. For trade between any state and any other state and at any time necessarily has political implications, and political judgments enter into decisions regarding it. When the British government moved in the 19th Century toward a free trade system, the underlying consideration was the advantage Britain would gain over its less developed rivals and hence the improvement that would follow in its relative power position. Other countries, including the United States, have traditionally and as a matter of course restrained, manipulated, or promoted foreign trade —in whole or in part and with friend and rival alike—as this seemed likely to enhance basic economic strength and national power. England's Adam Smith and America's Alexander Hamilton stood at opposite ends of the pole as to the kind of decision governments ought to make about foreign trade. But they stood side by side with respect to the purposes to be effected. Each saw as the end of policy added national strength. The difference between the two lay in the stage of development and the resulting needs of their respective countries.

Foreign trade, in short, is ordinarily and commonly an element of politics. Countries have used foreign trade to further the varied aims to which politics are directed: to build strength absolutely and relatively; to weaken an adversary or strengthen a friend; to attract and hold allies; to induce desired policy decisions by others; to secure, in other words, advantage for itself as a nation and as a power center.

Primacy of Political Consideration
Under Current Conditions

The use of foreign trade for political purposes is not necessarily limited to times of extraordinary international stress, or to situations of active hostility between two or more nations. However, when the vital security interests of a state are involved, political considerations logically become overriding. Certainly in the face of a broad and dangerous power confrontation, the governing criterion is the safety of the country. Given the communist commitment to strive by every feasible means to overpower the United States and to extend the communist system on a world scale, we have no choice but to shape our foreign trade policies, like all other policies, to the requirements raised by this menace. We must make such use as we can of the resource offered by foreign trade policy either to overcome or to dispel the menace.

The Problem of Using Foreign Trade as an Effective Instrument of Policy

We cannot expect to produce decisive results through such an effort. Foreign trade is not that sort of instrument. History, including our own history, is replete with instances where excessive reliance has been

7

placed on trade manipulation to attain specific foreign policy ends. Even when nations are closely interdependent, possibilities are severely limited, whether the aim is to weaken or to pressure or to establish a peaceful rapport. As between the United States and the communist countries regardless of what policies we or they adopt, interdependence of course is and will almost certainly remain minimal. The economies simply do not complement each other. But this does not mean we should write off one of the greatest nonmilitary resources available to the United States.

Given the economic power of the U. S., given the dominant position of the United States in world trade, it would seem almost axiomatic that foreign trade can be made to serve as a useful instrument of policy in dealing with the communists, irrespective of what may be the practices of other nations, either friends or adversaries. This might best be through continuing or even extending the practice of trade denial. Or it might best be through abandonment of trade denial in favor of using trade as a bargaining counter or as a means of otherwise attempting to influence the conduct and attitudes of communist states. The matter of choices, however, cannot and should not be faced up to at this point in this study. It can and should be faced up to only after consideration of a wide range of complex and interacting factors. What we need to be concerned with at this point is not what the U. S. should do, but how we should go about insuring that whatever the U. S. does do will be designed to support and further basic national objectives.

Chapter Three

THE PITFALLS

What do we want to accomplish through our East-West trade policy, whether changed or unchanged? What is realistically possible and what vain to attempt? What point can there be to postulating a policy that depends upon a requirement that clearly cannot be obtained under existing world conditions? Or a policy that demands for effectiveness a presupposed response from an adversary that is most unlikely to be forthcoming? Or a policy that contains elements which because of built-in circumstances must negate itself? Or a policy that would defeat other equally important policies?

These are elementary questions but very basic. Yet they are often forgotten or brushed aside. Discussion and studies to date reveal a strong tendency to disregard the limitations under which we must operate, or to proceed up blind alleys, or simply to stray or be led off target. In

8

several particulars, cautions are especially important. Specifically, there are some four major traps we need to avoid, traps that lend themselves to confusing issues and traps that can be all the more enticing because they are often self-baited. The four in question are:

1. *Exaggerated Expectations Regarding the Capability of the U. S. to Alter Unilaterally the Present Situation*

Sight is frequently lost of the fact that the United States is *not* a free agent when it comes to determining whether trade between itself and the communists is or is not to be liberalized, or is or is not to develop in this or that particular direction. U. S. restrictive policies are seen as alone responsible for the existing state of trade affairs; any move by the United States toward liberalization is looked upon as a sure means of bringing about a "normalization" of trade between the United States and noncommunist countries.

Such views, of course, are simply not valid. Except for those communist countries against which the United States maintains a total or near total embargo, the major determinant of trade relations between the United States and a particular communist state, including especially the USSR, is not policies of the United States but the policies of the communist state itself.

United States restrictive policies for the nonembargoed communist countries of East Europe apply only to a narrow range of goods available for purchase in the United States. The European communists are free to buy in the billions in the American market—if they wish to and are able to pay. This is not to say that U. S. restrictive measures are of negligible importance. On the contrary, they bear particularly heavily on the type of goods the communists are most anxious to buy; they significantly affect ability to pay; they inhibit businessmen who deal in unrestricted type goods from seeking trade with the communists; and the very fact that restrictions are applied to certain categories of goods reduces the attractiveness of the American market for goods in categories that are essentially free, so long as the same goods are available in other markets.

However, the controls maintained by the United States against the East European countries pale in comparison with the total controls maintained by those countries themselves. For the communist countries, total trade control is built into—is an integral part of—the over-all system. Any trade transaction, from the smallest to the largest, involves a political decision and constitutes a political act. Given a judgment by

9

the ruling authorities that this or that trade relationship, or this or that particular deal, is not to their political interest and does not serve in some way their political objectives, then the relationship or deal is simply and flatly ruled out.

We speak of building our East-West trade to certain levels; of controlling its content; of limiting it to goods "required for peaceful purposes"; of subjecting it to certain conditions. But what actually happens is not for us alone to decide. The communists will have their say. They have their own interests and objectives, and, as will be shown in some detail, these are quite different from our own.

Similarly, it does not lie in the power of the United States to condition trade in a way that will produce the type of over-all relationships between states and peoples that we may wish. It is easy enough to assume that trade by and of itself will necessarily lead to better understanding between ourselves and the communists, or will lead with surety toward a gradual transformation of communist societies in consequence of increased contacts, greater awareness of the benefits of our way of doing things, and the strengthening of those sectors of the communist economies which we believe will make for less totalitarian societies. However, we can be sure of none of these things. Where countries have kindred political and social systems, trade does not guarantee peaceful relations, or prevent explosive hostility. With the communists, results are even less certain. In the final analysis it will be communist policies and not U. S. policies that will determine what, if any, are to be the impacts of greater trade with the United States. These are hard realities of life that if ignored can only lead to confusion and misdirected efforts.

2. Targeting on Allies

Probably no other single factor has served so to confuse thinking with regard to U. S. restrictive policies than the far freer trade of our allies with the communist countries. This holds true for those who would adhere staunchly to restrictions as well as for those who would change them. In the case of both groups, the tendency is to think in terms of absolutes or nothing. Neither group, in effect, allows for the possibility of the U. S. producing significant results through its own efforts alone. The champions of restrictions would simply "make" U. S. allies conform to U. S. practices, even at the cost of effectively destroying the whole structure of the alliance system. Those who would have U. S. policies changed base their argument principally on the fact that the allies rather than joining with the U. S. are busy building an increasingly profitable trade, allegedly at U. S. expense.

Senator Karl Mundt argued at the Senate Foreign Relations Committee hearings that if worse came to worse and the allies continued their course unchanged we might find it necessary simply to shift targets:

> "It is not for us to capitulate but to continue to try to lead, not to become a follower. The fellow who has spent one hundred billion dollars trying to help the free world suddenly should not become a steam calliope at the end of the parade. We ought to continue to be out in front with the brass band trying to lead. Now let's not surrender; that is all I am asking. Let us try something. I am asking that . . . somebody call a trade-aid conference of the free major exporting countries of the world of which there are less than ten and get them together . . . and say: 'Look, this is a world problem, this is a free world problem. Obviously, if you are going to continue to expand your trade in everything that the Soviets want at the lowest and cheapest prices and at the longest and easiest terms of credit eventually Uncle Sam has to get into competition with you. And friends, we are still the biggest and the toughest and the strongest economic power in the world and if you are sure that what you want is this kind of competition, to see who can help the communists the most, and you force us, we can sell them so many more supplies than you are selling them and you are not going to benefit very much over the long pull.' "

The simple fact is that there is nothing new about the policies our allies are following, and no greater reason exists now than at any time over the past decade to let their practices determine what we ourselves shall do. Our allies have never seen eye to eye with us with regard to the efficacy of a restrictive policy. Contrary to what is often now said, Western Europe and Japan did not fall fully into step with the United States even during the early days of U. S. restrictions. They cooperated, and still cooperate, in denying to the communist countries a small range of goods of direct military or military-industrial significance. But aside from this minuscule of goods, they have always insisted on buying and selling from the communists freely. Occasionally, under conditions of acute crisis, or in response to extraordinary U. S. pressure, some but seldom all of the allies have moved to a reluctant and temporary tightening of their policies. But these instances have been exceptions to the general pattern that dates back to the end of the Korean War.

The spectacular increase since 1959 in the trade of other free nations with the communist bloc, and particularly with the communist countries of Eastern Europe, has not been a consequence of a new and greater willingness of those countries to sell, but of the communist countries to buy. No amount of cajolery, inducements, pressures, or threats on the part of the United States has succeeded in altering the attitude of the allies. Therefore, for overriding emphasis to be placed upon what other western countries are doing is to distort the pros and cons of the usefulness of the U. S. policy of restrictions. It goes without saying that U. S. policies would be more effective if they were fully supported by all other industrialized countries. But it does not follow that because such support is lacking, U. S. policies are to be judged an automatic failure.

Neither should a change in U. S. policies be called for simply because the other industrialized nations have not gone along with the United States. It is understandable that both those who argue for a change and those who argue against it are irritated with the other free nations which seek trade with the communists. But such irritation should not be allowed to obscure the variety of other considerations that need to be weighed in evaluating U. S. policies or in determining where the U. S. should go from here.

3. Overemphasis on the "Military Capabilities" Issue

One of the underlying objectives in the adoption of restrictive measures by the U. S. was to deny the communist countries, particularly the USSR, western technology that would contribute directly to the development of military capabilities. But this was far from being the sole objective. The more important purpose, in fact, was to deny the communists any significant assistance in their over-all efforts to expand their power base. This was implicit in the Congressional act that provided for an export control system, and it was made explicit in subsequent amendments to that act, most far-reachingly in the amendment of 1962. Despite this, however, there has been a growing tendency to measure the effectiveness of the control system on the basis of its effect or lack of effect on the growth of communist military capabilities.

Since it is quite evident that the communists' advance in weaponology has in no discernible way been retarded by our restrictive policies, this has had the effect of making any argument in favor of those policies an exercise in absurdity. As a matter of fact, if ability to hold back communist advances in weaponology had been put forward as the sole justification for restrictive measures when they were first under consideration, objective factors should even then have weighed strongly against adoption of the measures. For by late 1949, the USSR was known to have already succeeded in exploding an atomic bomb, and to be far along in its frenzied efforts to modernize its armed establishment across the board, including mechanizing its ground forces, putting its air forces on a jet propulsion basis, establishing a far-flung radar net, and making giant strides in rocketry.

As things now stand in the military sphere, probably the least "strategic" of all the goods that might be traded between the U. S. and the USSR are weapons of war, or products and technology related to weapons of war—although it goes without saying that neither side is going to engage in such trade. And even though either side would be delighted to get its hands on almost any item of military hardware from the other, to take it apart, to study it, and perhaps even to copy it, that would hardly affect the balance of military power, even if the buying process went only one way.

From the standpoint of the communists, and here one must think primarily of the USSR, far greater power benefit would derive from the import of a wide range of products and technology and know-how in areas of weaknesses in the economy than from the import of military products. The most "strategic" items the Soviets could import under present conditions would relate to agricultural production and to the chemical industry. For example, it has been suggested that the most valuable single bit of technology the Soviets could get from the U. S. would be the know-how and back-up equipment of the American poultry industry. And while the benefits would be strategic only in the sense of a contribution to the general economic well-being of the nation they would, in a variety of ways, increase war-making capability.

In this connection it might be instructive to recall the Soviet choice of U. S. goods under Lend-Lease during World War II. Compared with today, the Soviet arms industry was primitive and pressures for all types of weapons were infinitely greater. Yet the Soviets turned their backs on a wide range of U. S. arms including tanks, armor plate, non-self-propelled artillery, etc. in order to have more shipping space for trucks, tires and tubes, alcohol, canned meats, varied fabricating materials, precision instruments, metal working machine tools, petroleum products, etc. By the third year of the war, Soviet interest was far greater in the sinews of America's peaceful economic might than in its military arsenal. The clamor and pressure were directed toward petroleum refining equipment, complete chemical plants, natural gas pipeline equipment, precision instrument plants, machinery for the automation of the coal industry, and an endless variety of machine tools, presses, hammers, electric furnaces, locomotives, communication and railroad signaling equipment, etc. In comparison, guns and planes and even such a sophisticated military item as radar equipment were almost overlooked.

The point here is twofold:

. . . It is essentially meaningless to talk about a denial of trade in "strategic goods" with the European communist bloc in terms of weapons or other items of direct military importance; goods of true strategic importance range far beyond the direct military; moreover, they are constantly changing in nature and in relative importance.

. . . Therefore, for the U. S. to deny "strategic goods" to the communists with any degree of assurance would require a complete embargo of all goods. Even then, the U. S. would have to recognize the war-making capability of the communists would be only marginally affected, except perhaps for a very prolonged conflict.

What then is the meaning? Simply this: The military element has loomed far too large in U. S. thinking about trade relations with the communist countries. It has tended to override or to obscure all other considerations. On the one hand, it has furnished the yardstick by which effectiveness of established policies is measured; and, on the other, inhibited the flexible use of trade or trade denial as a broad-ranging instrument of U. S. policy.

The U. S. cannot now, and never really could, hope to cripple the communist bloc militarily by its restrictive measures. But it does not follow from this that trade and trade relationships are unimportant and do not significantly contribute to over-all U. S. strategy against the communists. In thinking about forward U. S. policy on trade, therefore, it is essential to focus on the possibilities of attaining greater effectiveness in the broad area of general strategy rather than to keep sights on ephemeral aims regarding military hardware.

4. Confusing Objectives

At its inception the U. S. restrictive policy was aimed exclusively at the USSR, with other communist countries lumped in because they were subject to control from Moscow and thus served to augment Soviet power. Inherent in the policy, therefore, was an implicit contingency allowance that if any of the communist states broke with the pattern of hostility toward the noncommunist world or otherwise moved toward the norms that govern relations among members of the free world community, the restrictive measures would be modified accordingly.

Thus, Yugoslavia was largely excluded from the provisions when they went into effect. Subsequently, similar though less sweeping exceptions were made for Poland, and quite recently for Rumania. On the other hand, when Communist China, North Korea, North Vietnam,

14

and, at the end of the 1950s, Cuba translated their hostility toward the noncommunist world into acts of aggression against free world positions, the intensity of the restrictive measures against them was stepped up to the point of virtually complete embargo. This flexibility in the restrictive policy was designed to insure that it could be used purposefully in support of U. S. objectives. In the words of Secretary of State Rusk, it was designed to insure that our policy would not serve simply as a blunt instrument against communists generally, but would be adaptable to requirements raised by changes in the policies and actions of particular countries.

Much of the discussion of our trade policies obscures or ignores this purpose. On the one hand, some insist that no distinction can safely be made between communist countries, while others argue that the guiding distinction between communist states should be whether a country is pursuing acts of overt aggression against the free world.

Thus, Communist China, North Korea, North Vietnam, and Cuba are placed in one category, while the USSR and the countries of Eastern Europe are placed in another. In the case of the first category, the general line is that there can be no thought of a relaxation of restrictive measures. In the case of the second category, relaxation is viewed as in order on an across-the-board basis since none of the countries in question is actively engaged in overt acts of aggression against U. S. and free world positions.

The effect of this categorization, to be sure, is to avoid using our trade policy as a blunt instrument against communists generally. However, it substitutes two blunt instruments for one blunt instrument. Specifically, it obscures the purpose of the United States to differentiate between the USSR and those communist countries which depart significantly from the Soviet policy of hostility toward the free world. In a larger sense, it obscures the fact that the basic aim of the restrictive policy has always been either to induce a change in the policies of the Soviet Union itself or to reduce the power of the Soviet Union to do harm to members of the free world community.

Chapter Four

THE MAIN TARGET: THE USSR

It is this matter of by-passing, or getting off focus, or misjudging or subordinating needs and possibilities with regard to the Soviet Union that generally must be our gravest concern. For the Soviet Union remains the pivotal element in the global challenge communism has thrust upon the United States. While Communist China, Castro's Cuba, and the varied other non-Soviet manifestations of communism's design to effect a revolutionary transformation of the world pose special dangers to the interests of the United States, the USSR is the keystone in the struggle against us. It alone has the power to make the struggle global and to threaten the security of the United States itself. Moreover, there is general agreement that no change should be made in U. S. policy toward Communist China, North Korea, North Vietnam, Albania, and Cuba. The consensus seems solidly for the continuation of a U. S. embargo both for now and in the foreseeable future.

Our Stated Purpose Toward the USSR: Struggle Until Freedom Prevails

The fundamental purpose of the United States with regard to the USSR is not only to successfully defend against its aggressions and encroachments, but to bring about somehow and sometime an end to those aggressions and encroachments and an end to the policies and world outlook from which they spring. This purpose has been the theme of an unbroken series of authoritative statements made over almost two decades, on behalf of four successive national administrations. The present Secretary of State Dean Rusk who has voiced the purpose on a variety of occasions, said at the convention of the Veterans of Foreign Wars in Minneapolis on August 13, 1962:

> "We have a simple but transcendent goal. It has been stated many times and in many ways. It is, in President Kennedy's words, 'a peaceful world community of free and independent states, free to choose their own future and their own system so long as it does not threaten the freedom of others.'
>
> "This goal of ours—and of most of the nations of the world—and the communist goal are incompatible. This global struggle will continue until freedom prevails. It goes without saying that our purpose is to win.
>
> "One hears now and then that we have a 'no win' purpose or policies. That simply is not so. Of course we intend to win. And we are going to win. . . .
>
> "Our hope and purpose is to win without a great war and the damage which the weapons of today would inflict upon the human race. For we will defend our vital interests and those of the free world by whatever means may be necessary, but a military climax to this struggle is to be prevented if possible."

To Win Without War

How to effect this victory without a successful trial at arms? As we

16

contemplate this question we must begin by recognizing two hard and basic facts about the Soviet Union; and we must treat these facts as central in any appraisal of the policies we are now following or any we may plan to follow in the future:

1. Soviet Dedication to the Destruction of the United States Continues Unbroken

The Soviet Union, by its own choosing and as a matter of deliberate design and deep-seated commitment, is now, as much as at any time in the past, engaged in a relentless and all-pervasive struggle against the United States. The object of this struggle has been well summarized by Khrushchev in his famous "we will bury you" assertion; its origin and nature are described by Secretary Rusk: "The struggle is a direct expression of the announced determination of the Sino-Soviet Bloc to extend their 'historically inevitable' world revolution by every available means. It is a program of action . . ."

The Soviet leadership, including the current leadership, has never attempted to hide its intentions. Indeed it has flaunted them. Yet myths about these intentions are increasingly the vogue. The Soviet Union is cast in a new character and one that ill fits either its stated aims or its conduct. It is seen as somehow more responsible than other nations, even U. S. allies—as ready and willing to join with the United States in a big-brother partnership in the world if only the United States can come up with a formula to quiet its suspicions and unlock its good intentions. The Cuban missile venture is conveniently forgotten; the test-ban treaty is inflated to watershed proportions; President Kennedy's June, 1963 American University address that suggested the United States might end the Cold War by changing its own attitude is viewed as a realistic basis for action.

The problem we face here has been well, if satirically, appraised by a British student of Soviet affairs, Ronald Hingley, a teacher of Russian Literature at Oxford. In the April, 1964 issue of Survey, Mr. Hingley wrote that the trend of public opinion regarding the Soviet Union had "produced a recurrent nightmare to which I am subject":

> "In the nightmare I am sitting somewhere in darkness, unable to move or speak. Opposite me a strange figure, more man than sheep, sits with a spotlight playing on its face. This creature (for some reason called 'Osric') is vaguely bleating as if seeking self-expression. Osric, on closer examination, is seen to be a sort of Anglo Saxon cream-faced loon with a great beaming, moonlight, pasty, hairless face. Gradually the bleats which issue from his slackly flexing jaws merge into a series of peristaltic, grunting pulsations, and words begin to be distinguished:

17

'understand the Russian point of view,' 'sincere,' 'cordial,' 'coexistence,' 'the Soviet man in the street,' 'what the Russians are thinking,' 'consumer goods,' 'destalinization,' 'trend towards liberalization.' I know that Osric is in danger and try to warn him. But before I can find my voice he is lassoed and trots obediently off, amiably wagging his tail, to the castrating shed."

2. Soviet Hostility Toward the U. S. Inherent in the Soviet System

Secretary Rusk has said of the cold war: " . . . We did not declare it; we ourselves cannot end it . . . the cold war will end when those who declared it decide to abandon it. Otherwise, it cannot end so long as people throughout the world are determined to be free, to decide their own institutions, to control their own destinies."

The struggle of the Soviet Union against the United States and the hostility which underlies it are not the products of a given situation, or of a set of particular policies of a particular group at a particular period of time. They are the product of the Soviet system itself, in fact a major reason for that system. No genuine let-up in the struggle or diminution of hostility can be expected unless and until one or more of the basic elements that make the system what it is are changed. These elements are:

—A monopoly of power held by a self-perpetuating oligarchy, the *Apparat* or professional managers of the Communist Party of the Soviet Union; a monopoly of power that is not less real whether wielded by a collective or by a dictator acting for and serving the basic interest of that oligarchy;

—The use of this monopoly of power to effect within the Soviet Union (a) the subordination of all particular groups and all individuals to the oligarchy, to the end that its monopoly of power will be maximized and perpetuated, and (b) to so control the total of activities within the country as to expand constantly the power and the power-base of the state;

—A world outlook that presupposes, as historically necessary, division, hostility, and conflict between the Soviet system and differing systems;

—A set of policies toward other nations and peoples which reflects that world outlook, and which actively and continuously seeks in varying ways and at varied levels of intensity to gain advantage, and ultimately complete victory, for the Soviet system in the continuing and inevitable conflict with other systems.

Given these facts, we can have little hope of "buying," through trade concessions, a better relationship or a different attitude on the part of the Soviet Union. Neither can we hope to erode USSR hostility by a subtle intrusion of our own influence through a "normalization" of trade. We cannot even hope to normalize trade in any true sense. As things are, trade between the United States and the Soviet Union, whatever direction U. S. policy may take, will necessarily be part of the struggle between the United States and the USSR. The very nature of the Soviet system will see to that. The Soviets make no attempt to disguise this hard reality. They speak of trade between themselves and the United States and other noncommunist countries as an element in "peaceful coexistence," but at the same time they make clear that, as Secretary Rusk again has said, "peaceful coexistence means to them a continuing attempt to spread their system over the earth by all means short of the great war, which would be self-defeating."

From this situation flow the ground rules that must govern in the determination of our policy: We cannot use trade to bridge the gap between our own and the Soviet system. We can, however, use trade as a means of getting at the Soviet system, even as the Soviets would use trade as a means of getting at our own. To accomplish this we cannot treat trade policy as if it stood alone or off to one side. We must weigh it and judge it and decide upon it in the overall framework within which all of our foreign policy must operate—that is, within the context of an all-pervasive world struggle.

PART 2

THE POINT OF DEPARTURE

Where then should a review, or any reworking, of U. S. trade policy toward the communists begin?

It should begin with the recognition and acceptance of the limitations and demands imposed by the gamut of U. S. policies toward both the communist and noncommunist worlds; in others words, with the requirements imposed by basic U. S. international purposes and the strategic needs flowing from those purposes.

Chapter Five

TRADE POLICY AN INTEGRAL OF TOTAL U.S. FOREIGN POLICY

A tendency currently exists to treat the U. S. restrictive policy as something of an aberration in the totality of U. S. foreign policy; as having been born of considerations that did not govern other foreign policies; as, unlike other foreign policies, dating back to another era; as being basically incompatible with and disruptive of other foreign policies. Illustrative of this tendency is the suggestive phrasing of the statement quoted in the preceding chapter with which the 1964 Senate Foreign Relations Committee hearings on East-West trade were opened.

The fact is, of course, the U. S. restrictive policy is an integral part of an overall foreign policy package put together between 1947 and 1951, which was subsequently refined and extended as an answer to the threat posed by communist aggression. The restrictive policy was not something simply drawn out of a hat, or dreamed up out of whole cloth; it logically emerged from an unfolding broad design. It was not intended to stand alone, but to operate as one of a group of policies that were *collectively* expected to produce certain results. It was supplementary to and interrelated with those other policies on which its effectiveness depended, and to which in turn it was intended to contribute effectiveness.

This is not to say the restrictive policy is so interwoven into the over-all fabric of U. S. policy toward the communists as to make impossible its modification without the whole fabric falling apart. It is to say, how-ever, that proposals for modifications should be looked at in the context of the relationship the restrictive policy has to other elements in the overall fabric and account taken of the effects the modifications would have on those other elements, as well as on the fabric as a whole. It is also to say that the usefulness of the policy should not be judged alone by the particular results it directly attains, or fails to attain, but should be weighed by the successes and failures of the whole package of which it is a part.

Chapter Six
THE GRAND STRATEGIC DESIGN

The objectives of the overall foreign policy package, of which the trade denial policy is a part, have been publicly spelled out time and again. In simplest terms, they are:

To leave no doubt in the minds of the rulers of communist states that a resort to general war on their part would result in unacceptable dam-age to their own states;

To deny to the communists any further extension of their territorial rule by direct or indirect aggressions;

To secure maximum collective action among the noncommunist states of the world to meet and defeat any threat of communist aggression;

To strengthen noncommunist states of the world to the end that (a) they be able more effectively to resist direct and indirect communist attacks on or within their own borders, (b) they be able to contribute more effectively to the collective defense of the free world, and (c) they become constructive participants in a viable community of free world nations;

To check the extension of communist influence among noncommunist peoples and states through such means as propaganda, economic pene-tration, political subversion etc.;

To hasten the dissolution of the forced and unnatural communist empire in Eastern Europe through the use of all appropriate peaceful means to encourage, assist and reward movement on the part of captive states toward independent policies and courses;

22

To deny to the communists any lasting fruits from their conquests in Asia;

To induce the rulers of the Soviet Union to reduce and ultimately to abandon their hostility toward and attacks on the free world and its system through (a) denying them returns from their hostility and attacks, (b) insuring that their hostility and attacks are increasingly costly to them and their peoples as well as fruitless in results, (c) refusing to accord them equal treatment with other states so long as they continue their hostility and attacks, and (d) responding in kind to any genuine movement they might make away from their policies of hostility and attacks.

These several objectives are interacting and interdependent. They all fall within, and together add up to, a single design for achieving, in the words of the present Secretary of State, "a world-wide victory for freedom."

Chapter Seven

POLICY ELEMENTS OF THE GRAND DESIGN

On what concrete policy elements does this design, and the several objectives that make it up, depend? These range over a wide spectrum and involve deep, long standing, and often astronomically costly commitments. They include the Truman Doctrine of 1947 with its commitment of U. S. aid to nations resisting or threatened by communist aggression, or facing internal difficulties beyond their power to resolve; the Marshall Plan and its engagement of the U. S. in the whole task of European reconstruction; President Truman's "Point Four" of 1949 and the successive and ever broadening involvement of the United States in the modernization process in the underdeveloped areas of the world; the establishment of a world-wide system of alliances beginning with NATO in 1948; special arrangements with the Latin American Republics looking toward a joint defense of the Western Hemisphere against direct and indirect communist aggression; and Alliance for Progress.

They include also a twice repeated demonstration of U. S. willingness to engage its military forces in defense of a people under communist attack; a thrice repeated U. S. stand at the risk of global war against a communist effort to extend the sphere of Soviet or Chinese Communist power; the expenditure of hundreds of billions of dollars to insure continued U. S. strategic superiority, to maintain a U. S. ability to engage effectively in conventional warfare, and to better equip the U. S. and various besieged peoples to cope with guerrilla and other subversive attacks.

They include many and varied efforts to instill in other peoples an awareness of the nature and methods and purposes of communist operations; to meet the challenge of the communist ideological drive; to counter the thrust of communist propaganda; to induce peoples and governments to safeguard themselves against communist economic penetration, communist cultural infiltration, undue dependence on communist trade and aid; to build up resistance to communist divisive efforts and tactics.

They include the policy, begun with Yugoslavia in 1949 and carried forward with Poland in 1957 and with Rumania in 1964, of treating different communist countries differently, according to their demonstrated willingness and capability to move toward greater national independence.

They include policies aimed at constantly probing the willingness of the Soviets to abandon or modify obstructionist and hostile positions on particular issues, and to entice and pressure them into acts of genuine accommodation between systems: in the field of disarmament; regarding settlement of the German problem; in the field of cultural and scientific exchange; with respect to possible cooperative undertakings in space, the peaceful use of atomic energy, the solution of world health problems.

And finally the elements forming the overall policy package include the series of special policies having to do with trade with the communist countries and related matters.

Chapter Eight

NATURE OF THE TRADE POLICY ELEMENT

These special trade policies, which in this paper are designated by the simple term "restrictive," encompass:

(1) Prohibition under terms of the Johnson Act of 1934 of privately extended credits to the communist countries;

(2) The requirement under terms of the Exports Control Act of 1949, as variously amended, particularly by the Act of 1962, that all exports to communist and communist-dominated countries be subject to license, and that licenses not be granted for export to "an unfriendly nation" of any article or technology, "if the President shall determine that such export makes a significant contribution to the military or economic

potential of such nation or nations which would prove detrimental to the national security and welfare of the United States";

(3) The requirement through various acts that the U. S. seek the cooperation of friendly nations in the denial of certain types of goods to communist countries, and provision, through the Battle Act, for punitive action against nations endangering the common security through trading with communists;

(4) A denial of most-favored-nation treatment to communist countries;

(5) An embargo, on the basis of several acts, of any trade between the U. S. and Communist China, North Korea, North Vietnam, and Cuba (excepting for Cuba foods and medicines);

(6) The exception, by various acts, of Yugoslavia from most of the above restrictions;

(7) Similar but less inclusive exceptions for Poland;

(8) Limited Executive Department initiated exceptions for Rumania;

(9) The adoption of various administrative devices to safeguard against transshipment of prohibited articles to communist countries and to insure conformance with domestic practices of subsidiaries and branches of U. S. companies located abroad;

(10) Negotiation and establishment of a voluntary cooperative arrangement between the U. S. and NATO allies and certain other European countries and Japan whereby agreement is reached and common action taken with respect to the denial of exports to communist countries of direct military importance. (Operational machinery under this arrangement is provided by the "Coordinating Committee" (COCOM) of the "Consultative Group" of representatives of the cooperating countries.)

Chapter Nine

HOW THE TRADE POLICY ELEMENT FITS IN

These trade policies aimed, of course, at limiting for the communists the military and economic benefits that were presumed to flow from unhampered trade with the United States and other countries of the free world. But their purpose was not confined to this. The policies and the implementing measures were seen as important in a variety of ways in attaining the range of objectives that make up the grand design, or the overall strategy, of the United States in its struggle against the communist danger. And in actual practice the impact of the trade policies has doubtless been far greater outside than within the economic-military hardware sphere. They have, in other words, served principally to further and support varied political ends rather than to retard the economic and military progress of the USSR and the other communist states.

Symbolic Significance

The restrictive policy has come to serve, for example, as a major symbol of U. S. cold war resolves and purposes. It has manifested to the body of the American people, to the other peoples of the free world, and to the communists themselves, the intention of the United States to oppose the communists and their designs with every means at its disposal so long as communist policies and conduct threaten the United States and other free nations. It has clearly signaled that in the U. S. view communist purposes are irreconcilable with U. S. purposes and that the U. S. is willing to make continuing sacrifices to insure the defeat of communist purposes. It has demonstrated that the U. S. has no intention of according unregenerate communist states the same treatment and the same degree of respectability it accords nations not warring against it; that the U. S. sees the hostility of the communist states toward the world community of nations as precluding full and equal membership in that world community.

To Promote Dissidence Within the Bloc of Communist States

The restrictive policy has served also as the key to the U. S. policy of "treating different communist countries differently" in that it provides, essentially, the only concrete means through which the U. S. can encourage and reward communist states which show a will and an ability to adopt a less hostile and a more independent course. It enables the U. S. to demonstrate at one and the same time (1) implacable hostility to those communist states that remain united in hostility and aggressive purpose against the United States and the rest of the free world, and (2) a willingness to move to a different position and a different attitude as particular communist countries move.

To Alert and Safeguard Vulnerable Peoples

The policy has had a major role in U. S. efforts to forestall an extension of communist influence and power through techniques and devices aiming at economic, cultural and political penetration, followed by subversion and control, particularly with regard to the emerging and

26

developing countries. The policy has furnished the framework for a direct and continuing effort on the part of the U. S. to build up an understanding among the authorities of vulnerable countries of the dangers inherent in indiscriminate trade and related contacts with communist regimes, and to induce them to hold themselves aloof from such contacts.

These efforts have not, quite obviously, prevented a steady extension of communist "trade and aid" activities in developing areas of the world, excepting many of the countries of Latin America and a few in Asia. The efforts, however, have doubtless been instrumental in increasing the sophistication of the authorities in target countries, something that has resulted in a denial to the communists of many of the fruits they expected to derive from their activities. In any event, whatever success the U. S. efforts have attained has been importantly dependent on the fact that the U. S. itself practices what it preaches. Beyond this, the policy has given solid substance to the general political posture the U. S. has assumed in the less-developed countries with regard to the communist states. It has exemplified and dramatized the U. S. concern that every possible safeguard be maintained by all free countries against the various dangers engendered by communist machinations and drives.

Toward a More Effective Western Alliance

The restrictive policy has always loomed large in the U. S. design of building a more effective partnership among the North Atlantic nations. Initially, the hope was strong that an extensive program of trade denial could be agreed upon between the U. S. and its allies, and that this would lead not only to increased pressures on the communist states but also to significant forward movement in the development of cooperative activities, exchanges, and machinery within the alliance itself (that is, would extend the area of alliance concern into an added dimension).

This hope, of course, has been poorly realized. Others of the western states have viewed trade denial in an altogether different light than the U. S., and their cooperation has proved from the first both reluctant and minimal. Moreover, U. S. efforts and pressures to effect a change in attitudes have generated important frictions and irritations between the U. S. and even the closest of its friends. Nevertheless, in U. S. relations with the allies, as elsewhere, the U. S. position on trade with the communists has dramatically symbolized and given body to the overall U. S. policy of holding the line against the communists.

No Rending Competition

Of a different order, but perhaps even more significant, has been the

27

fact that the U. S. policy has minimized friction-breeding competition between the U. S. and its allies over the East European market. While doubtless a strange-seeming source of strength for a mutually beneficial alliance system, what this has meant in practice is indicated by the bitterness produced in U. S.-Canadian relations by the sale beginning in 1957 of large quantities of U. S. wheat to Poland for local currencies. The Canadians complained, and quite understandably, that this was a type of competition in which they were not equipped to engage.

What would have been the effect on other of the allies, and on the whole North Atlantic system, if the U. S. over the years had used its vastly superior resources to undersell, in one manner or another, all others in the Eastern market? And what will be the effect if the U. S. proceeds, as some urge, on an underselling operation in the future? Former Secretary of State Christian Herter in December, 1961 told a House Subcommittee on Foreign Economic Policy: "I can think of nothing that the Russians would like better than to see a first-rate trade war between this side of the Atlantic and the other side of the Atlantic." Secretary Herter was thinking at that time of a trade war in free world markets. But this prognosis would hardly be less accurate in case the trade-war was over markets within the communist world.

Direct Impact on the USSR

With regard to the Soviet Union itself, the role of the restrictive policy is dualistic: It serves at one and the same time as a stick (actual) and a carrot (potential). On the one hand, it constitutes one of the costs the U. S. is resolved to impose on the USSR so long as its aggressiveness and hostility continue; on the other, it represents an area in which the U. S. can afford to move in case the USSR gives convincing evidence of a genuine change in its own policies and attitudes.

Chapter Ten

EFFECTIVENESS OF THE TRADE POLICY ELEMENT

How well does the restrictive policy serve our strategic design? What is the actual impact on the communist countries, most notably on the main target, the USSR? These are key but extremely difficult questions. Obviously, the policy has not produced and is not now producing all the desired results. It has clearly failed in certain specific things expected of it. But the same can be said of any of the *individual* elements that make up our total policy against the communist threat, for example,

28

assistance to developing countries or even our alliance system. In the final analysis the only way in which the individual elements of our strategy can be proven out is on the basis of how well the strategy itself is working.

Nevertheless, we can and should single out our trade policy and do our best to approximate its effectiveness. In the case of this policy, unlike some others, there are alternatives that we might well adopt, alternatives in fact that many are *urging* that we adopt.

We do not have a great deal to go on in performing this task. And what we do have is principally inferential.

Soviet Attitude Toward the U. S. Restrictive Policy

An obvious test is the reaction of the target. What does the "squealometer" show? Over the years, the USSR has made much of U. S. restrictions. It has denounced the measures as "discriminatory," as indicative of U. S. preoccupation with the "cold war," as an "obstacle to the relaxation of tensions," as incompatible with the principles of "peaceful coexistence." The Soviet leaders have urged abandonment of the policy, have avowed an interest on their own part in the establishment of good trade relations with the U. S. "on the basis of equality and non-discrimination," and in the rapid expansion of trade in both directions.

How genuine is this stated Soviet concern? Some suspect it is but a vehicle for propaganda against the U. S. And indeed Moscow has missed no opportunity to make propaganda capital from the U. S. restrictive system. Spokesmen have exploited from all angles the contrast between what they call the U. S. "trade boycott" and the avowed willingness of the Soviet Union to engage in "mammoth" trade with the United States regardless of "differences in social systems"; they have, among other things, tried with all the skills they could command to use this contrast to "prove" the U. S. fears to engage in "economic competition between systems," because of its "awareness" of "the superiority of the socialist system."

Beyond the Calls of Propaganda: Nevertheless, the USSR's expressions of displeasure over the U. S. policy and of its interest in having the policy changed in favor of a better trade relationship and a greatly increased volume of trade almost certainly represent more than a propaganda gambit. The nature of the propaganda treatment itself strongly suggests this. And, far more important, there is the matter of Soviet arguments, approaches, and overtures in serious private conversations with official and unofficial representatives of the United States, at various levels.

It has been a rare occasion on which a Soviet leader or spokesman has engaged in serious talk with an American about the possibility of a relaxation of tensions, the need for better U. S.-Soviet relations, the chances of settling outstanding issues in dispute, or some other such matter without introducing the problem of the present state of trade relations and the desirability of the U. S. abandoning its restrictive measures. Almost as if by formula, the Soviets have invariably contended that the first step in any general or partial improvement in relations between the United States and the USSR has to be the placing of trade on a better footing, that is, the ending of U. S. "discriminatory policies." After that, the argument goes, would follow not only massive Soviet orders for U. S. products but also a steady improvement in the political climate, and, by implication, perhaps the settlement of some of the major issues in dispute between the two countries.

Khrushchev in particular showed almost an obsession over U. S. trade policies. In meetings with Eisenhower and Kennedy, in off-the-record interviews with American correspondents, on occasion of receiving new U. S. ambassadors, in meetings devoted to negotiation over critical issues, Khrushchev's beginning point was almost always the problem of trade and the U. S. restrictive policy. He harangued about it, pleaded against it, joked about it, stormed at it, and openly puzzled over it.

Motivation of Soviet Campaign Against U. S. Policy

Why is it that the Soviet leaders have shown such great concern over this one policy of the United States? Why is it that they have concentrated so much attention on getting it changed? Why have they put so much stress on a trade relationship that has rarely in times of peace produced a two-way turnover of goods amounting to as much as $100 million in a year?

A sure answer to those questions would provide the best of all guides for the determination of the kind of trade policy toward the communists that would best serve the interests of the United States as against the USSR. A sure answer cannot, of course, be found. Nevertheless, there is much in the indirect evidence that bears on the puzzle which needs to be given great weight in our thinking and planning for the future.

Perhaps the key to an answer lies in the assured confidence of the Soviet leaders that the laws of history, together with their complete mastery over the Soviet trade structure, guarantee that if the U. S. would but engage in trade, the USSR would come off the better for that trade. In other words, by the simple refusal of the opponent to play, they feel they are being beaten at a game that they are superbly equipped to win.

30

Facetious as this way of putting the matter may appear, it cannot and should not be summarily dismissed. Meanwhile, however, there are a number of particular points that bear upon the problem.

The Economic Factor

First there is the matter of economic impact. The standard Soviet line has been that while the Soviet Union would like to trade with the U. S. it is capable of taking care of its own needs and suffers no ill effects from the American "boycott." Often a claim is added that the denial of products from the United States has actually been beneficial to the USSR, since it has brought the development of industrial capabilities that might otherwise have been neglected. But other evidence, including statements made in private discussions, indicates a more serious Soviet view of the economic consequences than statements made for public consumption .

The Trade That Might Have Been: Particularly noteworthy is the practice of the Soviet leaders to talk in terms of a mammoth trade level between the United States and the USSR, once U. S. policies have been changed. They speak again and again of the possibility of billions of dollars of Soviet orders for U. S. machinery and equipment. While this talk aims in part to serve as a lure, it seems also to reflect a genuine hope if not a real expectation. In this, the Soviets appear blissfully ignorant of, or at least unwilling to accept, the hard economic realities that will necessarily govern U. S.-Soviet trade. The responsible factor may well be memory of Lend-Lease days when complex industrial machinery and equipment and the most sophisticated and advanced products flowed virtually at command from the United States to the USSR. An element of mysticism in regard to U. S. economic capabilities appears also to be involved. The Soviets still manifest a deep admiration for U. S. productive power. And they appear to believe that if the doors to U. S. production can but be swung open, a great boost will be given Soviet efforts to fulfill its still distant economic goals.

The Matter of Technology: U. S. technology is of course at the heart of the matter. Soviet imports from abroad aim at securing for the USSR the best in the way of technology that is available. Denied access to the advanced technology of the United States by the restrictive policy, the Soviets cannot be sure that they are in fact getting the best in the way of technology when they make purchases abroad. Should they be able to pick and choose between U. S. technology and that of other industrialized nations, Soviet buyers might well in many instances take a non-American item in preference to an American. Lacking an opportunity to compare, however, the Soviets can never be sure when they make a purchase abroad that they are not being forced to settle for "second best."

Indicative of Soviet thinking about what U. S. technology and U. S. technical and industrial know-how could mean to Soviet development, was Khrushchev's "shopping list" letter to Eisenhower in 1958. In this letter Khrushchev spoke of:

> "Purchases by the Soviet Union of industrial equipment in the United States, including complete equipment for plants and factories; conclusion of agreements with firms for obtaining licenses in individual cases; inviting American specialists to work in Soviet enterprises as consultants on the production of certain synthetic materials, and for acquainting Soviet specialists with the production of these materials and finished articles thereof. . . .

> "Organization of meetings of American and Soviet scientists and specialists for discussing problems of production of synthetic materials. . . . Mutual participation of Soviet scientists in the work of scientific research institutions of the United States of America, and of American scientists in the work of scientific research institutions of the USSR regarding new types of synthetic materials and technological processes. . . .

> "At the same time the Soviet Union could propose a broad program for placing orders in the United States for other types of equipment and for the production of consumer goods, and for housing and public construction, for refrigeration equipment; installations for air-conditioning; equipment for the cellulose paper and wood processing industries; the textile, leather footwear, and food industries; television equipment; equipment for the manufacture of packing material; packing, packaging and automatic vending machines; pumps and compressors; machinery for the mining industry, for the manufacture of building materials and the mechanization of construction; hoisting, transporting, and other equipment. . . .

> "In addition . . . big orders could be placed for a number of industrial materials and finished products including orders for equipment for rolling ferrous metals. . . ."

Additions to Industrial Plant: Soviet interest in securing machinery and equipment from the United States, and indeed from the industrialized nations generally, arises of course from the fact that it offers a short cut to the realization of industrialization goals. At times, and this would include the past several years, the Soviets place heavy emphasis on additions to their capital plant. In the case of a number of selected industries, the Soviets appear either: (a) to lack the ability to develop necessary plant facilities on their own, even where western prototypes are available for copying; (b) are propelled by a sense of urgency that makes

32

them unwilling to take the time necessary to develop and build plant facilities; or (c) prefer simply not to divert human and material resources from one developmental operation to another. For these selected industries, therefore, the Soviets seek to secure complete plants from abroad. Currently included among such industries are the petrochemical, chemical fertilizer, textile, artificial fiber, food processing, and plastics. These industries are in areas which have been traditionally neglected in the USSR, and they are also in areas in which the United States occupies a very advanced position.

Stopgaps and Prototypes: Generally, however, the Soviets do not go in for outright additions to their capital plants. Rather they concentrate on securing machinery and equipment from abroad that can both (a) fill in while Soviet capabilities to produce the items in question can be developed, and (b) serve as a prototype for copying purposes. Over time, it has been in this manner that the USSR has drawn principal benefit from its imports from abroad. When the Soviet leadership begins to develop a new industry it frequently asserts its intention to rely heavily on imports for the complete plants or at least the specialized machinery and equipment needed for the industry. Yet there is no instance where once a start has been made in any industry that imports were not first reduced and then virtually cut off, with Soviet products being substituted for those from abroad.

This happened in the case of the hydroelectric industry, the steel industry, the automotive industry, the petroleum refining equipment industry, the precision tool industry, and on and on. It remains to be seen whether this past pattern will be repeated for the chemical, plastics, artificial fiber, etc. industries, in which so much emphasis has been placed on massive foreign procurement in recent years. The chances would seem overwhelming that it will; and that after a tremendous build-up of "order-expectations," the Soviets and not the British, Germans, and Americans will be the source of the "billion of dollars" of equipment required for these industries over the long term. As a matter of fact evidence is already accumulating of a sharp decline in purchases abroad in support of these programs. (This may, however, be due to the tightening gold-foreign exchange situation rather than to a decision by the Soviet leaders that with the help already received from foreign sources, the Soviet industrial establishment is now in a position to pick up and carry on.)

General Importance of Imports to Soviet Development: Just how important imports from the West have been to the industrial development of the USSR to date, or how important they will be in the future, is difficult to determine. If reliance is placed upon the statistical relationship of the imports to GNP, or to total investment in industrial plants, the importance will appear very small indeed. Total Soviet imports from the industrial West ordinarily represent a fraction of one percent of Soviet GNP. However, use of such a crude statistical method for determining the significance of imports, particularly with the highly selective nature of Soviet procurement abroad, almost certainly leads to a gross underestimation of the role of imports. A far better indication lies in the nature of the items involved and the sense of urgency that invariably marks Soviet procurement. The Soviets themselves have, in other ways, given ample evidence that imports have been a prime element in past industrial progress, and that imports loom quite large in the industrialization plans for the future.

If it is difficult to judge the importance of the West as a whole to Soviet industrial development, the problem is compounded for the U. S. alone. Generally speaking, the role of the U. S. has not only been less than that of Western Europe but of several individual West European countries, particularly Germany and the U. K. Equipment from the United States was relatively important for the first five-year plan, as were U. S. engineers and technicians who worked under contract in the Soviet Union. And certainly U. S. shipments under Lend-Lease were of far-reaching significance. From the standpoint of vastness of quantity, the advanced technology embodied, variety, usefulness as prototypes, and almost any other criteria, the "civilian-type" tools, equipment, complete plants, machinery for almost every conceivable purpose, instruments, etc., received by the USSR under Lend-Lease constituted a bonanza for Soviet development that is almost without parallel. That the postwar "carry-over" of Lend-Lease industrial items—most of which were intended for developmental purposes when they were procured—played a tremendous part in industrial reconstruction and development in the postwar years is certain. And very likely their importance continued through many more years after reconstruction was completed.

The U. S. Market and the Drive for Efficiency: But the economic significance of the U. S. market in Soviet eyes is not necessarily related to any specific role the U. S. has played in the past or is realistically likely to play in the future. As a factor in the Soviet calculus, the U. S. market has weight in accordance with what the Soviets think or believe about it. And here the mysticism noted above may be quite important. Further, it is possible the U. S. market is looming larger and larger in Soviet minds for the simple reason that Soviet development has reached a stage where it requires, above all else, a steady increase in efficiency.

How to attain this efficiency? Soviet commentaries suggest great and relatively desperate soul-searching over the question. And as the focus on efficiency has intensified, the lure of the U. S. market must surely have grown correspondingly. For, to the Russians, perhaps more than to any others, American production is synonymous with efficient production. What the Soviets would want and expect from the U. S. market would not be just particular American machines or plants embodying the most advanced technology, but American *production* technology—with technologically advanced machines combined with a variety of other elements that also represent advanced technology, both in themselves and in the interrelated way they are utilized in American enterprises. The Soviets may feel, as well they might, that their future progress depends not upon getting more and more individual machines, but upon the massive import of technology in this broader sense, the massive import of a peculiar *amerikanski* technology.

The Main Impact: Political and Psychological

Completely aside from the question of the economic effects of U. S. restrictions and of the part these have played in generating Soviet reactions, the restrictive measures have demonstrably had an important political and psychological impact.

Soviet Political Sensitivity: In virtually every discussion of the subject by a Soviet leader, from the beginning on, a deep feeling of sheer political affront or even outrage has quickly shown through, seemingly overshadowing every other consideration. The reason for this seems clear: at the very time the USSR has been going all out to assert and secure acceptance of its status as one of the two great world powers, fully equal to the U. S. as a force in world affairs and with the right to an equal voice and equal consideration by all other nations, the United States has disdained it as a trading partner, has dared to "discriminate" against it, has treated it as a "second-class citizen."

Khrushchev gave a typical demonstration of this sensitivity in the course of an important discussion with a representative of the U. S. in 1959. He reacted violently to a statement that the Soviet Union could, without any change in the U. S. restrictive policy, buy great quantities of goods in the United States, including machinery and equipment for plants to manufacture shoes, synthetic fibers, etc.

Khrushchev's irritated answer was that this was not the issue. He did not need to turn to the United States to learn how to make shoes or sausage. He was solely interested in the ending of "discriminatory practices" directed against the Soviet Union. He was interested in the general

35

principles of trade with the United States. He would welcome it if the United States were to rescind discriminatory practices. That the United States should be unwilling to do this would mean that it wanted a continuation of the cold war which, regrettable though it was, would not disturb the USSR. The Russian spirit was strong and would hold out in that situation. Any offer to the USSR of such items as shoe lasts was insulting to the people of the Soviet Union. The Soviet people know how to make shoes, he boasted, perhaps even better than the Americans.

Khrushchev's whole concentration was on the discrimination issue as such. He insisted he was not concerned about trade itself but rather about principle, about the Soviet Union's right to trade. The problem of trade, he asserted, was more political than economic. Some people in the United States wanted the Soviet Union to buy chemical products from them; this was totally unrealistic. Some people still did not realize that the Soviet Union was a grown-up nation, that it could even build such things as the United States had not yet been able to build. The approach of the U. S. was highhanded and amounted to a policy of carrying on the cold war. This policy had failed in the political field and it would fail also in the economic field. The Soviet Union was a strong nation; it could hold out. The Soviet Union wanted to trade with the United States; but such trade would have to be on the basis of equality and without injury to the national pride of the Soviet people. Any attempt to impose conditions on the Soviet Union would fail.

Upset of the Soviet Doctrinal Calculus: A factor that doubtless compounds Soviet political outrage over the U. S. restrictive policy is that it runs counter to everything the Soviet leaders believe about a nation "dominated by monopoly capitalists." As noted below, in the Marxist-Leninist book, capitalists are supposed to put their search for profits above all else. In the Kremlin's eyes the Soviet market should be most attractive to U. S. business. Wall Street, the presumed master of the country, should long since have laid down the law to the government in Washington and under no uncertain terms. That it hasn't done so violates the Soviet sense of the order of things. The leaders feel cheated of their just due as communists dealing with capitalists.

The success, limited though it has been, that the U. S. has had in inducing the rest of the capitalist world to go along with restrictive measures, adds fuel to the flame of Soviet indignation. This again violates very basic principles, those that relate to the irrepressibility of contradictions among capitalist countries as a result of rivalry over markets.

Coupled with this puzzled feeling of somehow being tricked by capitalists not acting as they are supposed to act, appears to be a persistent

36

belief among the Soviets that once trade between the United States and the USSR has gotten under way on a new basis, the capitalists of the United States would revert to type, as the communists see the type. The Soviets might then expect, as in Lenin's day, sympathetic understanding and support from those carrying "order books." These would be concerned to keep good U. S.-Soviet relations and might be expected to throw their weight against anti-Soviet adventures and policies on the part of the U. S. government, and in support of measures that would make for bigger and better trade. Illustrative of this kind of reasoning was Khrushchev's expressed conviction that once a new start had been made in U. S.-Soviet trade, the United States would soon come around to the granting of large-scale credits. For in his words: "Sometimes one who grants credits is more interested than one who obtains them."

Chapter Eleven

A MISSING LINK?

From both the political and the economic sides, then, the U. S. restrictive policy sits very ill with the Soviets. It may not actually hurt them very much—that is a matter that can only be left to conjecture, probably for the Soviets as well as ourselves—but it irritates and bothers them; it has the frustrating impact of any barrier that is beyond their own power to do anything about; and it denies them the assurance in their economic management and planning that would come from easy access to the world's greatest seat and source of economic accomplishment and power. The Soviets strongly desire to have the policy away and done with.

This reaction is in part explainable in terms of the standard Soviet stance regarding trade with noncommunists. The Soviets may or may not want to trade with the U. S. at any given time. But they want to be free to trade if and as they see fit, if and as the trade serves their own purposes. Both their theories and practices call for a flexible use of trade in support of basic policies; and for such use to be made of trade, the way for trade has to be open. Otherwise, obviously, no Soviet initiatives will be possible.

Yet there are elements connected with the reaction that strike a discordant note, that suggest a real hurt and a special vulnerability. Four of these elements more or less stand out:

1. The policy is peculiarly disturbing to the Soviets. It upsets their whole scheme of things. It doesn't fit into expected patterns. It means

37

the USSR, which itself seeks to be a missile, is faced with a moving rather than a standing target.

2. Reaction is disproportionate to its evident cause. Evidently, the weight of the policy is magnified by a mysticism that goes with the thought of "what might be if it could be."

3. Aside from other considerations, the political impact of the policy —the stigma it places on Soviet prestige and the affront it constitutes to the Soviet sense of national pride—causes the Soviets to attach substantial importance to its elimination simply for the sake of eliminating it.

4. In the final analysis, the most important factor may be that, because of a variety of deep-seated reasons, the USSR's plans to carry its developmental process to its ultimate conclusion, that is to a point of superiority over the U. S. and to the point necessary for the support of the heralded "communist society based on plenty," have gone very much awry. A search is quite evidently on to find ways and means to break out of the present binds that are holding back the building of a capability for production "in abundance." This search is fanning out in many directions, including some that would lead to more of the same that has prevailed in the Soviet Union in the past. But also included is a hesitant exploration of the possibility of trying to work into the Soviet system some of the elements on which western progress depends. And as these explorations take place, eyes are magnetically drawn to the U. S. and to what the U. S. market, in its broadest meaning, offers.

What are the meaning and the implications for the United States? Are there openings for the U. S. to make more effective use of trade, and trade denial, in its overall strategy? Is there need to extend the role of the restrictive policy so as to make possible a more flexible and active approach for positive purposes?

As the policy is now structured and administered, it can be played in only two keys. Given static cold war conditions, it automatically follows that restrictions are to be rigidly applied. In other words, in a situation of continuing confrontation between the U. S. and the USSR, the very role of the policy as it is now structured requires that the U. S. give no ground. For, should the United States give ground under this circumstance it would be voluntarily sacrificing one of the more important of the "costs" it is capable of inflicting on the USSR for its hostile attitudes and conduct.

Equally automatic would seem the requirement for a relaxation in the policy: In a situation of cold war movement, that is in a situation where

38

the USSR gave convincing evidence of an intention to change its policies and conduct in ways that would bring it closer to the norms maintained within the world community of nations, then almost by definition the U. S. would not only have less reason to inflict "costs" on the USSR, but would want through trade, as well as through other means, to nudge the USSR forward in its movement.

Thus, as things now stand, the whole question of how we use trade is not a matter for decision; it is open and shut according to which of two circumstances prevails: As long as the Soviet Union remains "bad," restrictions are applied full force; when the Soviet Union becomes "good," then the reasons for restrictions fall away and the policy changes.

But is this adequate to meet the strategic needs of the United States under current conditions? Many argue that it is not. They view the restrictive policy as it is now structured as more of a stance than a true policy. They see it as adequate only within a strategy of "containment." In the case of containment, the underlying concept was that if the United States and the remainder of the free world simply held the line against the communists and denied them any benefit from their aggressive efforts, meanwhile forcing them back onto themselves, the results would inevitably be the automatic onslaught of degenerative forces that would ultimately bring about either the collapse of the ruling elements, or a forced change in fundamental policies. All that this concept required of the United States was negative policies aimed merely at "denial." Thus, it would have been entirely consistent with that policy for the United States simply to sit tight with its restrictive policies unless and until the communists in one way or another came or were brought to heel.*

---

* The basis of the expectation under the containment concept that the Soviets could be brought to heel with only negativist U. S. policies is suggested in the following extract from the famous "X" article on "The Source of Soviet Conduct" which appeared in the July, 1947 issue of *Foreign Affairs,* and which first publicly aired the concept: "All of this, both the maintenance of internal political security and the building of heavy industry, has been carried out at a terrible cost in human life and in human hopes and energies. . . . To all that, the war has added its tremendous toll of destruction, death and human exhaustion. . . . In these circumstances, there are limits to the physical and nervous strength of the people themselves. . . . In addition to this, we have the fact that Soviet economic development, while it can list certain formidable achievements, has been precariously spotty and uneven. . . . It is difficult to see how these deficiencies can be corrected at an early date by a tired and dispirited population working largely under the shadow of fear and compulsion. And as long as they are not overcome, Russia will remain a vulnerable, and in a sense an impotent nation, capable of exporting its enthusiasms and of radiating the strange

But a pure containment policy did not long serve, if it ever served, as a basis for the U. S. strategic design. Beginning at least with the Eisenhower Administration and continuing on through the Kennedy Administration and into the Johnson Administration, it has been the avowed purpose of the United States not simply to rely on historical forces to bring about desired changes within communist ranks. At times, the aim had been toyed with of actively using pressures to force changes, as in the case of project "liberation." At other times, and this was true of the Eisenhower Administration as well as of the Kennedy and Johnson Administrations, the thought has been to make positive efforts, when and as suitable opportunities offer, to induce changes.

Against this background, it might well be that something is needed beyond a flat "either-or" stand with regard to U. S. trade policies toward the communists. There may be a need for a link that would enable the United States to bridge the gap between using trade policy to inflict costs and using it to encourage movement already convincingly under way, that is to use it to get movement started in a situation of inactive stalemate. The point is that the United States might fruitfully seek to utilize in a more direct and active way than in the past the resource it possesses in its economic power, and in the context *not* of an assumed "state of peace" with the USSR, but of continued hostility and even struggle.

The Soviet leaders avow that "economic competition," in which they allow an important place for expanding trade, can well serve them in their continuing struggle against the United States—in other words, that it constitutes an instrument through which they can further their cold war aims. There is no reason why the United States for its own part cannot seek to utilize trade as an instrument to further its cold war aims, that is to achieve victory in the great conflict the USSR has thrust upon it. For the United States to do this successfully, however, will require utilizing—not scrapping—control of trade. There can be no thought of abandoning either of the dual roles which the present trade policy serves. Rather, the aim will need to be to supply the missing link between these roles. Any change in the restrictive system should be in the direction not of simply yielding ground but of replacing one line of action with another. And unless and until the USSR comes virtually full circle toward rejoining a world community of free states, we should always stop short of granting it the type of trade relationship we maintain with present members of that world community.

---

charm of its primitive political vitality but unable to back up those articles of export by the real evidence of material power and prosperity."

40

How to devise such a missing link? How to use trade as a positive instrument of struggle so long as struggle continues to be forced upon us? How to use it better to further, and not to abort, our strategic design?

In these questions the point of departure is to be found for any review or revision of our present trade policies toward the communists. To move from this point of departure to a successful solution of the basic problem will require skill, adroitness and ingenuity. The ground for maneuver open to us is narrow not broad. We have to deal with a moving, not a standing target; with an adversary that will make every effort to turn our own aims and designs against us. And special and complex problems will always have to be kept in mind and dealt with. We cannot assume that through some magic we can transform realities through the policies we decide upon. We have no choice but to accept that, for any policy to be effective, it must be both rooted in reality and designed in such a way as to capitalize on reality.

PART 3

ECONOMIC STAKE OF THE U. S. IN EAST-WEST TRADE

Chapter Twelve

THE QUESTION OF ECONOMIC COSTS VS. GAINS OF RESTRICTIVE POLICY

A recurring theme in the current commentary on U. S. policies and East-West trade is that the costs to the U. S. far exceed the gains. It is argued in most of these instances that at the time of the adoption of the restrictive policy, it made economic as well as political sense in that it promised to avoid the necessity of more expensive alternatives, since:

(a) The outright aggressiveness of the Soviet Union under Stalin was creating conditions of near war which not only justified but required all feasible actions on the part of the United States and other free nations, including a resort to economic warfare measures, to discourage and counter this aggressiveness;

(b) The relative inferiority at that stage of the USSR as against the United States in strategic weaponry gave reason to believe the denial of trade with the West would retard the development of the war-making capability of the USSR and hence the likelihood that the Soviet leaders would risk engagement in war;

(c) The general economic backwardness of the USSR would enable the western countries, particularly the United States, through trade denial to force a significant slow-down in the modernization process within the USSR, and with that to bring pressures to bear on the Soviet leaders to change their attitudes and conduct; and

(d) Economic isolation of the newly established Soviet Eastern Empire would have the effect of a forced turning of the communists inward, leaving them to stew in their own unsavory juices.

Need For a New Balance Sheet?

With the great changes that have taken place since the inception of

43

the restrictive policy in 1949, the argument continues, the situation has become altogether different. The crude aggressiveness of the Stalinist days with its threat of imminent war is now a thing of the past; the Soviet Union, without benefit of trade with the United States, has built a modernized armed establishment which includes all the components that are available in the United States; the USSR has made such giant strides in building its own industrial base and its own technological superstructure that it is now beyond the capacity of the United States to exert more than a nuisance influence on Soviet economic development; and, to ice the cake as it were, all other industrialized countries have long since dropped their embargo policies except for items of direct military significance and have opened the way for the USSR to procure from them virtually any item that is denied by the United States.

Meanwhile, the market offered by the USSR and the other countries of Eastern Europe has become increasingly important, with purchases in the West already ranging in the billions of dollars per year, with the prospect of added billions in the future. The restrictive policy has thus, the argument runs, become more the policy of denial to the United States than to the communist countries. While the communists are being made to suffer inconveniences, American business interests, and indeed the very economy of the nation, are suffering huge losses.

It is certainly in order that the question of costs as against gains, in a direct economic sense, be given great weight in the consideration of any particular foreign policy being followed by the U. S. It may well be, in fact, that given the peculiar type of conflict the communists have forced upon the United States—that is a struggle in which staying power is all important—the outcome will be decisively influenced by the success one or the other of the contestants has in selecting strategies and weapons that are more costly to its adversary than to itself. Certainly, the communists consider this factor of the utmost importance. The very foundations of their strategy of selected, controlled, and indirect aggression is to insure that the enemy is always presented with a choice of either yielding a position or resisting in ways that will maximize his costs, while those of the communists are minimal.

A Picture of Staggering Trade Opportunities

Also, it must be acknowledged that with regard to the substantive argument, surface evidence does suggest—or perhaps better, the surface evidence makes it easy to convince oneself—that the self-exclusion of the U. S. from the eastern market represents a substantial and growing loss to both the U. S. business community and the U. S. economy.

For one thing, there is the spectacular increase in the trade of the communist countries with the industrialized countries of the West— primarily Western Europe and Japan—an increase that proceeded at the rate of roughly 15 percent per year between 1958 and 1963, and an absolute increase from $3.7 billion in 1958 to 6.2 billion in 1963.

Then there is the matter of the astronomical figures thrown about by the communist leaders. Khrushchev's talent for expansiveness was, for example, never more evident than when he was holding out the lure of massive Soviet orders for western products, including especially products from the United States. Thus, in his "shopping list" letter to President Eisenhower in 1958, he proposed a trade between the USSR and the United States "of several billion dollars . . . over the next several years," and he went into great detail as to the specific categories of goods the Soviet Union would want to buy. And this was but one of a number of Soviet avowals of a willingness, even a strong desire, to transform trade relations with the U. S. from a state of abysmal paucity to overflowing plenty, and not alone by Khrushchev.

While doubtless subject to some discount by nearly all observers, these glowingly depicted prospects of vast new trade opportunities have quite evidently had a substantial impact on wide circles in the United States. It is thus not surprising that serious groups of business leaders have come to talk of a level of trade between the U. S. and Eastern Europe equal to that of the West European countries, something that would mean a two-way turnover of some $6 billion a year, compared with an actual turnover that averages less than $100 million.

Quite obviously, trade possibilities of this magnitude, if they should be real, would be of great moment to a variety of particular American interests and to the nation as a whole. To continue to close the door on such an opportunity through a deliberate policy of trade denial would quite obviously involve serious sacrifices or costs for the United States. To be sure, few Americans would complain of the costs if it were clear that substantial results were being achieved in the way of furthering the nation's foreign policy objectives against the communists. If, however, the resulting gains for the U. S. should be only marginal, complaints of a "bad bargain" for the United States would be both understandable and justified. "If the cold war is to continue," a sensible person might well be expected to say under this circumstance, "let it continue, but let us fight it in ways and with means that hurt the adversary more than we are hurt. Where we, rather than the communists are suffering the greater damage, as in the case of this trade denial policy, let us back up and start over again."

45

Chapter Thirteen

A CASE OF FAULTY ESTIMATES
AND ILL-FOUNDED HOPES

Is this what the situation really is? Is the United States blindly following a policy that costs it billions a year in trade, to achieve purposes that are no longer attainable?

The question of what the policy is achieving may well be debatable. But it must be said that trade opportunities of the magnitude suggested above are grossly exaggerated, or better, grossly distorted.

Built-In Drags on Communist Trade with Noncommunist Countries

Perhaps the most fundamental thing to recognize when speculating about long-term trade relations between communist and noncommunist countries is this: so long as the communists remain truly communist, built-in factors will operate to guarantee that their trade with noncommunists will generally be at a level far under what would prevail in the case of trade between capitalist countries of comparable economic strength. Frequently estimates are made of trade possibilities with a communist country like the USSR on the same basis that they would be made for a noncommunist country that is, on the basis of gross national product, rate of growth, developmental plans, etc. This is simply not sound. The communists themselves explain the reasons for this again and again.

1. *Economic Isolation a Strategic Dictate*: As a matter of principle, the communists seek economic isolation between themselves and the noncommunist world. They consider economic self-sufficiency as a strategic necessity in view of the "history-dictated" irreconcilable conflict between their system and all other systems. At the same time, as is discussed in the next section, they see in a policy of trade denial on their own part, that is, in the withdrawal of their markets from "capitalistic exploitation," one of the surest means open to them to bring about the ultimate defeat of capitalism.

2. *Autarky not Trade the Basic Aim*: As a matter of both principle and practice, which is departed from only rarely and then because of special and transitory circumstances, communists limit trade with capitalist countries to only such items as are required to meet developmental needs. The basic aim of foreign trade, communist economists explain, is to eliminate the need for foreign trade. The procurement of

46

machinery and equipment needed to build productive capacity is the main focus of all communist trade efforts. And for the most part, it is machinery and equipment for new industries, with orders building up during the ground-laying period and then tapering off almost to the vanishing point once the new industry is firmly established.

To take the case of the USSR as illustrative: During the first five-year plan major emphasis was upon equipment needed for the steel industry, hydroelectric stations, tractors for the mechanization of agriculture, and varied machine tools. In the late thirties, a shift took place to petroleum industry requirements and to tools and materials needed for the manufacture of tools and equipment for complete plants. After the war, it was coal mining machinery, complete plants for the manufacture of precision instruments and complex tools of varied kinds, equipment for the aluminum industry, advanced petroleum refinery equipment, and complete chemical plants. In the stepped-up "surpass the U. S." drive that began in the late fifties, petrochemical plants and equipment were the major targets; to these have recently been added chemical fertilizer plants and plants for plastics and synthetic fibres.

Even during the war, Soviet purchasing agents were heavily preoccupied with the procurement of developmental items, sometimes at the expense of meeting immediate war needs.

The concentration of the Soviets on developmental items has had the effect not only of greatly narrowing the range of their import activities, but of generating great activity in certain fields at certain times, followed by an almost complete fall-off of interest. The Soviet Union once offered one of the West's greatest markets for steel-fabricating equipment; it has long ceased to be a major purchaser in this field. The same story has been repeated for oil drilling equipment, petroleum refinery equipment, precision instruments, coal mining machinery and equipment, machinery and equipment for automobile manufacturing assembly lines, etc.

3. *Neglect of Means of Payment*: The whole developmental scheme of the communist countries allows no place for export industries as such. As exports are required to finance the purchase of developmental items abroad, they are, in effect, simply scrounged for. Nothing could underscore this point more sharply than the fact that as of 1964 the composition of Soviet Russia's exports to Western Europe and other industrialized countries is almost identical to that of Tsarist Russia's exports. This, among other things, places a severe limitation on the ability of the communist countries to finance heavy purchases abroad on any sustained basis.

In the case of the Soviet Union, for example, a great flurry of foreign purchases is invariably followed by a period of very low activity, making the Soviet market one of the most uneven in the world. Thus, the massive purchases of the first five-year plan period and of the first two postwar years quickly dwindled to very small proportions. And the last eighteen months have produced suggestive indications that a strong decline is under way as against the great acceleration that marked the 1958-63 period. The hard, and highly important, fact is that given the nature of the economic structure of the communist countries, the capacity to pay for goods from abroad on a continually expanding basis is simply lacking.

Variations from the Standard Pattern

For some of the communist countries one or another of the above generalizations does not always apply, or applies only in part. Thus, communist China over a period of several years has followed the very uncommunist practice of focusing its foreign trade activity heavily on the purchase abroad of grain required for immediate consumption; also, the regime seems to be trying to restore China's traditional export industries. There can be no certainty, however, that this pattern will endure. Indeed, the Chinese leadership asserts that its break with the communist norm is temporary and will be succeeded by a renewed industrialization and self-sufficiency drive. Be that as it may, the importance of the Chinese market, notwithstanding wishful thinking to the contrary, is currently so small that it makes little difference in an economic sense what the policy of the Chinese communist regime is.

Several of the East European satellites are also not closely following the standard communist pattern. In their case, a new factor has been introduced in the desire of the ruling regimes to reduce their economic dependence on the USSR. Consequently there is a tendency on the part of these countries to put their trade relations with the West, particularly with Western Europe, on something of a "normal" basis. Again, however, the economic consequences are not likely to be great whatever policies they follow.

If the volume of East-West trade is to be built up to any considerable extent within the next generation or so, the USSR will have to be the key. And in the case of the USSR each of the limiting factors noted above applies full force, which means that Soviet foreign trade activity almost certainly will be low when compared to the potential suggested by its gross national product and its relatively rapid rate of growth. It also means that Soviet foreign trade activity will almost certainly be decidedly uneven.

Chapter Fourteen

ADDED LIMITATIONS OPERABLE ON TRADE WITH THE U. S.

The foregoing sobering points apply to trade of the communist countries with the West generally. When it comes to the particular problem of trade with the United States, further inhibitors are at work. The level of trade between the United States and Eastern Europe has always been extremely low, both in relative and absolute terms. Except for the two world war periods, the volume of exchange has been but a fraction of that of Western Europe. Even during the desperate first five-year plan drive of the Soviet Union for machinery and technology from abroad, most Soviet orders went to Western Europe and not to the United States. And since the wind-up of Lend-Lease and UNRRA transactions, trade between the U. S. and the European bloc has been all but negligible.

While this in part has been due to deliberate policies of the governments on each side, the major cause has without question been the fact that the United States and Eastern Europe economies do not complement each other. Only where U. S. aid efforts shore up trade transactions, as in the case of Yugoslavia and Poland, do exchanges between the United States and individual communist countries equal a level worthy of statistical note within the overall accounting of U. S. foreign trade. Except for this one factor, the total of U. S. trade with Eastern Europe is about at the level of the turnover within a major U. S. shopping center in one of the larger American cities.

Chapter Fifteen

HOW LIFTING U. S. RESTRICTIONS WOULD AFFECT THE OUTLOOK

In General Terms

Should there be a change in U. S. trade policy toward the communist countries to bring it into line with the West European, a substantial increase in trade would almost certainly take place. Percentagewise and over the short term the improvement could be expected to be quite great. There would doubtless be a flurry of backlog orders for U. S. products embodying technology superior to that available in Europe or Japan, or offering some other distinct advantage. But the total of all such products would be small indeed when compared with the volume of purchases from the other industrialized countries. And much of the buying would be nonrecurring. Similarly, the extension of most-favored-nation treatment to the communist countries—which would necessarily have to be part of the U. S. decision to relax restrictions if the relaxation were to have meaning—would yield some increase in U. S. imports from those countries and a corresponding rise in continuing U. S. exports. But again the quantities in both absolute and comparative terms will not be sufficient to raise substantially the general level of trade.

Probable Specific Range of Trade under the New Conditions

To put the matter in more concrete terms, the following points can be used as a basis for a reasonably realistic calculation of the possible range of U. S. trade with the communist countries on the assumption that all special U. S. obstacles to such trade (legislative, administrative, and psychological) are removed:

1.   With regard to *demand,* U. S. exporters under the assumed conditions could reasonably expect to secure a share of the East European market based exclusively on their competitive position as suppliers.

2.   A measure of what the competitive position of U. S. exporters would be is how well they do in the West European market, since their competitors in this market are the same as they would face in the eastern market.

3.   In other words, the U. S. share of the East European demand for particular categories of goods should be roughly equal to its share of the West European.

4.   Three-fourths of East European imports from the industrial West consist of (a) machinery and equipment, and (b) metals and metal manufactures.

5.   The U. S. in 1962 (the latest year in which all figures necessary for this calculation are available) supplied 16 percent of Western Europe's imports of machinery and equipment, and 6 percent of its imports of metals and metal manufactures.

6.   It is therefore assumed that without its special obstacles to trade with Eastern Europe the U. S. in 1962 could have secured the same percentage of East European imports of these same commodity groups. This would have meant U. S. exports of machinery and equipment and metals and metal products amounting to *$190 million in 1962.*

7.   It is usually assumed that imports of the East European countries from the industrial West will increase in the years ahead by a rate at least equal to the rate of growth of the gross national product of these

countries. Assuming this rate will average 5 percent per year, which may well be on the high side, and applying this rate to the U. S. share of the East European market indicated above, then U. S. exports to those countries of machinery and equipment and metals and metal manufactures would *in 1970 total $267 million.*

8. As an outside limit, but one that still would not be out of line with the trend of the past eight years, East European imports from the industrial West might increase by an average of 10 percent per year. In that case, U. S. exports of these two categories of goods would *in 1970 total $420 million.*

9. U. S. exports to the East European countries of commodities other than machinery and equipment and metals and metal manufactures amounted in 1962 to approximately $100 million. However, some three-fourths of this total consisted of agricultural products provided Poland under P. L. 480 and other special arrangements. Since no determination can be made of what the U. S. may or may not do about the continuation of these subsidized exports to Poland (although it would seem most unlikely that the U. S. will steadily increase them), it is impossible to estimate with any degree of exactness the level of U. S. exports of goods in this "other" category by 1970. As an outside possibility—and for varied reasons probably a highly unrealistic one—it might be assumed that the ratio of imports of goods of this type to total imports by communist countries from the United States would be the same as for the industrial West as a whole. In that event, it would mean adding 25 percent to the anticipated imports from the U. S. of machinery and equipment and metals and metal manufactures.

This would result in *total imports from the United States in 1970* of approximately $334 million assuming imports of the East European countries increased at the rate of 5 percent per year; or *$500 million,* assuming they increased at the rate of 10 percent per year. This then would be the range of East European imports from the United States, taking into account only the demand side: from *$334 million to $500 million.*

The foregoing quite obviously represents a very rough calculative process. Yet it probably furnishes as sound a basis as any for a realistic estimate of the range of possible East European demand for American goods in case the U. S. brings its restrictive system into harmony with that of the countries of Western Europe. Certainly this process, crude as it may seem, is far more dependable than one that involves projections based upon planned programs of industrial and agricultural expansion, GNP, rates of growth, or claims and lures put out by communist leaders.

Singling out the Soviet Demand for U. S. Goods

This calculated range, it is important to stress, has to do with the European communist bloc as a whole, that is, it applies to the USSR and the European satellites combined. But what of the situation with regard to the USSR alone? For several reasons prospects for U. S. trade with the USSR need to be broken out and looked at separately:

1. The USSR is at the center of—is indeed the prop for—current speculation that a massive volume of trade can be built up between the U. S. and the communist countries of Eastern Europe. Figures are ordinarily lumped together for all of these countries, but the focus is on the Soviet Union and its assumed great demand for western goods: that is, focus is on the already established economic strength of the USSR, the projected rate of growth of the Soviet economy, and the stated aim of the Soviet leadership to rely upon an increasing volume of western exports in its efforts to carry out ever more grandiose developmental plans.

2. Politically, the USSR and the East European satellites constitute entirely separate targets. The U. S. already has a policy of liberalizing trade with the satellites if and when there is good prospect that this will lead to the assertion of greater national independence on the part of the governing regimes of those countries. If considered desirable, this policy could be broadened to the point of almost complete liberalization of trade relations between the satellites and the United States without necessitating any change in U. S. policies directed toward the USSR, or as a matter of fact. without any particular bearing, one way or the other, on those policies. This, moreover, would be but the continuation on a new scale of established U. S. purposes. With the USSR the matter is different. The USSR poses the real issue that is at stake in the present discussion. And for it, entirely different economic as well as political considerations govern.

3. Contrary to what the situation was several years ago it cannot be simply taken for granted that the same trends will prevail in trade relations between the European satellites and the West, and the USSR and the West. Political motivations and purposes underlying trade vary greatly; there is a differing pattern of requirements; foreign trade plays a much larger role in the smaller economies of the satellites than in the economy of the USSR; the strength of traditionalism is far greater in the former than in the latter; so also is affinity for the West.

4. By far the most important point is that, in terms of projections based upon the current situation and the trends of the past several years,

the satellites and not the USSR offer the best prospect for expanded foreign trade. These subpoints need to be noted:

a.   As of now, the satellite grouping and not the USSR constitutes the major element in trade between the Soviet communist bloc and the industrialized countries of the West. While the Soviet Union does most of the talking and commands most of the attention, it is the lesser communist countries that do most of the trading. Thus of a total 1963 trade turnover between the European bloc and the industrialized West (excluding Finland) of $6.0 billion, the satellites accounted for $3.6 billion, or 60 percent, while the USSR accounted for $2.3 billion, or 40 percent. With regard to imports alone from the industrialized countries— that is, the "market" for western goods in the communist countries— figures in 1963 were $1.8 billion for the satellites and $1.1 billion for the USSR.

b.   Getting down to the specific case of the United States, prospects of trade expansion between the U. S. and the USSR are even appreciably less than the dim ones indicated above for the European bloc as a whole. (In other words, in the calculation made above the weight of the satellites was disproportionate to that of the USSR.) The situation with regard to machinery and equipment sharply underscores the point: There can be little question that if the U. S. is to appreciably expand its activity in the Soviet market, the principal ingredient in the expansion will have to be machinery and equipment. During the five-year period from 1960 through 1964, the Soviet Union placed orders for machinery and equipment in the industrialized countries of the West at an annual average rate of approximately $335 million. If, as was assumed earlier, the U. S. could capture the same share of Soviet imports of machinery and equipment as it now has of West European imports (i.e. 16 percent), then during the 1960-1964 period it could have sold an annual average of about $55 million of machinery and equipment to the USSR. Projecting this figure into 1970, assuming an annual rate of expansion of 10 percent, U. S. shipments of machinery and equipment in 1970 would be under $100 million. There would of course be other U. S. exports, but if past patterns mean anything they would be minor compared to machinery and equipment exports. (It might be instructive to compare this projected figure with Khrushchev's 1958 assertion to President Eisenhower that the Soviet Union was prepared to purchase goods from the United States, which would have consisted almost exclusively of machinery and equipment, totaling "several billion dollars . . . over the next several years.")

c.   If U. S. machinery and equipment exports to the USSR of less than $100 million by 1970 under liberalized U. S. trading policies seem absurdly low, it might be useful to note that Soviet imports of *all products* from its major western trading partners, the United Kingdom and West Germany, totaled in the bonanza year of 1963 $155.1 million and $153.6 million, respectively. For the three years 1961, 1962, and 1963, Soviet imports from these two countries combined were of this range: $324.7 million; $323.4 million; $308.7 million. And this for years in which Soviet trade with noncommunist countries was at a level far above what it had been in any comparable period in history.

Chapter Sixteen

OBVERSE OF THE DEMAND SIDE: THE PROBLEM OF PAYMENTS

Moreover, there is more to the story. However attractive U. S. goods may be for buyers in the Soviet market, there will always be a problem of payment. While communist resources are adequate to sustain a low level of imports or to cover a one-shot splurge of orders—even though scrounging is often required in these cases—the matter of financing is a very serious one for any sustained build-up of communist imports from the U. S. It is so serious, in fact, that it serves now, and will continue to serve until and unless fundamental changes are made in the basic system that prevails in the communist countries, as a built-in ceiling on the expansion that can be effected in trade between the communists and the U. S. To be specific, U. S. exports to the communist bloc at the lower end of the range given above, that is at a $334 million level, would be extremely difficult for the communists to take care of; U. S. exports at the upper end, that is at the $500 million level, would be all but out of the question. Several points need to be noted in this connection:

1. Exports of the European communist countries to the United States in 1962 totaled only $79 million: $63 million from Eastern Europe, and $16 million from the USSR.

2. The low level of these imports was due in part to factors rising from U. S. policies and attitudes. These factors include: the application of discriminatory tariff duties in consequence of the denial of most-favored-nation treatment; certain U. S. import restrictions; and consumer bias against products from the communist countries. However, the low level was due more importantly to the inability of the East European countries to produce substantial quantities of goods marketable in the United States.

3. The elimination of the U. S. restrictive system, including the granting of most-favored-nation treatment, would by itself enable an appreciable increase in the U. S. take from the communist countries, with, however, more of the benefit going to the satellites than to the USSR. Also, with the increased motivation that would follow from the greater opportunities to buy in the U. S., some improvement in the quality and variety of goods offered for the U. S. market might well take place. However, given the production pattern in the communist countries, particularly within the USSR, such an improvement would necessarily be marginal. Here, it is important to note, the situation with regard to the U. S. and Western Europe is entirely different, at least up to a point. The West European countries readily take the foodstuffs, crude materials, and petroleum which make up the great mass of the exports of the USSR and Eastern Europe. These products can only be sold on a small scale in the United States.

4. The hope exists in some quarters that an answer can be found to the payments problem in Soviet gold shipments or in a triangulation process through which Western Europe would pay for communist exports in convertible currency and the communists would pay for U. S. exports with the currency thus earned. However, such hope appears ill founded.

Regarding the Gold Possibility

Annual gold production of the communist bloc (i. e. the USSR) runs between $150 million and $200 million a year. And in the period since 1957—that is, during the time when the USSR and the satellites have so strongly increased their imports from the industrial West—gold sales have greatly exceeded production: for example, by more than two and a half times in 1963 and 1964, and by more than two times in two other years. Gold reserves have consequently fallen to a very low figure. In the case of the USSR, from roughly $3.0 billion in 1955 they have dwindled to something under $1.5 billion at the beginning of this year. Theoretically, gold shipments within the limits set by current production and the precarious reserve could be diverted from the other industrialized countries to the United States. However, this possibility is limited not only by the needs of the communist countries to continue to procure goods from Western Europe, including many items requiring a long lead time for manufacture that have already been placed on order, but also by the need for gold to finance chronic deficits on service accounts. Some small increase in gold production is possible and even likely over the next several years. But the quantities involved will not be sufficient to alleviate more than very moderately the payments pinch.

Regarding a Triangular Solution

Each of the other industrial countries carries on its trade with individual countries of the communist bloc under a bilateral agreement. Import surpluses are accepted in the short run, but remedial action is taken if they persist. Also, the communist countries of Eastern Europe are approximately one billion dollars in debt to Western Europe, most of it in the form of medium-term credits, and the debt is growing. Communist countries need, therefore, to build up export surpluses with their West European trade partners merely to take care of servicing these debts. For these reasons, the U. S. can hardly expect hard currencies to be available in any substantial quantities for the financing of communist purchases in the United States.

The Question of Credits

The communist leaders, and here reference is primarily to the leaders of the Soviet Union, have made clear they would hope, and expect, to finance expanded imports from the United States by means of extensive credits. In fact, on many occasions when the Soviets have spoken of the need for the U. S. to change its trade policies, they have by implication equated granting credits with the elimination of "discriminatory" measures. Ordinary commercial credits, even if government guaranteed and liberally interpreted so as to run for a longish "short-term" (e.g. up to five years), would not solve but only postpone the problem. Credits, if they are to serve as a basis for a substantially expanded U. S. trade with either the USSR or the other communist countries, must be long-term, that is, of the fifteen to thirty year variety.

It is such long-term credits, government-to-government in nature, the communists have in mind. But even if the U. S. did fall in with communist wishes for a long-time postponement of the day of reckoning through such credits, it is difficult to see how repayment could be made when it came due. So long as the communist countries continue to concentrate their resources and energies on the development of their basic industries and otherwise expanding their power base, they will be unable to find means to meet their current needs, much less to service long-term debts. Thus, even long-term credits would only serve to postpone and eventually to complicate the basic problem of payments. The communist leaders doubtlessly recognize this, but persist in their demands and hopes, evidently on the basis of their hallowed Leninist belief that the U. S. is so beset, or will become so beset, by the problem of surpluses that it is only a matter of time before it will be forced to resort to almost any extreme in order to get relief, including the extreme of going along with a subterfuge in order to virtually give goods away.

Export Industries

Assuming the U. S. will avoid any such slippery credit slope as the communists would have it get on, the only solution for the payments problem—the only way in which the East European countries can finance substantially increased imports from the U. S.—is for them to develop export industries capable of producing products that could find a ready market in the U. S. This, however, would require the diversion of enormous resources and energies from cherished developmental goods. It would, in effect, require a major shift in the long-set direction in which the communist economies have been moving. And it would risk a chain reaction that would have far-reaching repercussions on the very system that makes communist countries communist. We can be sure, therefore, that as long as the ruling regimes have freedom of choice, they will avoid such a dangerous course. And we can be equally sure that if the regimes do in fact stay away from export industries, their ability to pay for goods in the American market will be so constrained as to place a limit of some $300 million annual imports from the U. S.

Chapter Seventeen

THE PAYMENTS PROBLEM AND AN IMPORTANT SIDE ISSUE: COMPETING WITH THE EUROPEAN ALLIES

Many observers will no doubt quarrel with the assumption put forward that the United States will be able to do no better comparatively in the Soviet market, and indeed in the markets of the whole of Eastern Europe, than it does in the markets of Western Europe. In contrast to this particular assumption there appears a fairly pervasive assumption that once restrictive policies are eliminated, the U. S., because of its technological superiority and because of its general competitive power in the foreign trade field, will be able to take a leading position in trade with the communist countries.

A theme that runs through much of the current commentary is that the United States should be able to grab a share of the East European market at least as large as that of the other industrialized countries. That would mean that if East European imports from the industrialized West continue at the 1963 rate of $2.8 billion a year the U. S. could expect to obtain about one half, or approximately $1.4 billion a year. This would assume that the United States would be playing a rough competitive game, which many believe is not only justified but required. As was suggested in an earlier section, feeling runs along these lines:

> The other industrialized nations are allies of the U. S. They have a common interest with the U. S. in checkmating communist aggressive aims. Their own destiny is as dependent as U. S. destiny on the preservation of U. S. military superiority over the communist countries. They have an equal stake with the U.S. in winning the competition between systems. All have received costly support from the U. S. to build up and preserve their strength and viability as against the common enemy. Yet these nations actively push trade with communist countries. Why should the United States stand aside and permit this to go on any longer? Why should American businessmen be forced to yield a highly valuable market to their competitors? The communists are not being hurt, only American business. All the U. S. has done is to divert business to Western Europe. Therefore, why not limit the U. S. restrictive measures to those enforced by other industrialized countries and move to capture the rightful U. S. share of East European trade, thus raising U. S. trade to the level of the West European?

Obviously, a strong case can be made for the justice of a U. S. reaction along these lines. Unfortunately, however, the problem is not one of justice as against injustice, of fairness as against unfairness. It is a problem of realistic possibilities and consequences. Righteous indignation, even if understandable and whether directed at allies or at one's own government, is beside the point.

A Program of Subsidization?

If the U. S. is to engage successfully in competition with Western Europe for a substantial part of East-West trade, it must do more than end its "discriminatory practices," and more than bring to bear the competitive skills of American traders. The simple fact is that the West Europeans enjoy a decisive natural advantage in trading with the East; they are able and willing to accept in payment for their goods the products available in those countries for export. The United States, on the other hand, is not. The only way in which the situation can be substantially changed is for the United States, or individual U. S. traders, to offer concessions to the communists adequate to offset the natural advantage enjoyed by the West Europeans. Moreover, there must be a willingness to outdo the West Europeans in this subsidization game, which they are already playing to a certain extent among themselves, and which they would surely step up against the U. S. (To the West Europeans a competitive U. S. drive in Eastern Europe would raise an indignant query as to who is trying to divert whose markets from whom.)

There can be no doubt that if the United States should enter into a contest of this type, it would have the power to win it. It is indeed true, as Senator Karl Mundt pointed out in the statement quoted in an earlier section, that the United States is "still the biggest and the toughest and the strongest economic power in the world," and can well say to the West Europeans: "If you are sure that what you want is this kind of competition, to see who can help the communists the most, and you force us, we can sell them so many more supplies than you are selling them and that you are not going to benefit very much over the long pull."

The issue, however, is not whether the United States can outdo the Europeans in this type of contest. The issue is whether it would be economically beneficial and politically wise for the United States to enter into the contest in the first place. This involves the question of whether it is in the interest of the United States, from any standpoint, to throw its immense resources into a struggle with the other industrial countries for an "unnatural" share of the Eastern market. And it involves far more than a simple redress of the balance between the U. S. and its Western competitors. It involves the possibility of a vast extension of the opportunities open to the communist countries to derive advantage from Western trade.

How far can the U. S. afford to go in conceding advantage to the communists in order to outdo its allies? As much as one would like it otherwise, the U. S. cannot have the one without the other. It is not a simple matter, as some would have it, of the U. S. doing what everyone else is doing, with no greater or more serious consequences than are already being produced. There are built-in economic limits on what the communists can get from trade with the other industrialized countries of the West, regardless of how liberal the policies of the latter may be. With the U. S. and its vast resources aggressively in the picture the matter would be entirely different. The unpleasant policy choice for the U. S. is, therefore, simply this: whether to concede an unfair advantage to friendly competitors who refuse to budge from the course they have selfishly set for themselves, or to risk a dangerous advantage to an adversary.

Chapter Eighteen

BY WAY OF DISMISSING THE ECONOMIC FACTOR

In summary, it can be said that, realistically appraised, the economic stake of the U. S. in East-West trade is hardly likely to be substantial so long as communist systems as presently constituted and oriented continue their sway in Eastern Europe. This would be true even if U. S. sales were at the higher of the two possible levels calculated above, that is at the annual rate of some $500 million by 1970. But because of payment problems, sales at this level appear so unlikely as to call for ruling them out for anything but the most speculative purposes, Realistically, thinking must be in terms of a top ceiling of around $300 million of sales by 1970, and even this would be difficult enough to attain.

For certain elements in the American business community, particularly for machinery and equipment producers and foreign trade concerns, a step-up of U. S. exports to Eastern Europe to the $300 million level would be quite important. But for the nation as a whole, the economic significance would be quite minor. If everything else were equal, the gain, small though it would be, would of course have value. But everything else would not be equal. To build up even a $300 million export trade with the European communists would require the U. S. to accept goods which it does not particularly want or need, to grant credits which even if kept within a five-year limit would certainly produce headaches and problems, and perhaps to enter into a sharp and repercussion-producing competition with its allies.

The conclusion must be, therefore, that from the strictly economic standpoint, and of course in terms of the nation as a whole and not individual traders, the benefits that would flow from a change in the U. S. restrictive policy would be so marginal as to make the light hardly worth the candle. And this despite all of the grandiose schemes and dreams that it is possible to conjure up during flights of fancy.

This conclusion leads to a second: Economic considerations as such need to be given scant weight in the determination of what the U. S. should or should not do about its trade policy toward the communists. Political considerations and political considerations alone should govern. Given the slight economic stakes that would be at issue whichever direction final decisions take, the U. S. can safely proceed with an attempt to devise and apply a trade policy that will best serve its strategic objectives without need for concern over the consequences for its own economy.

PART 4

FROM THE SOVIET STANDPOINT: SOVIET THEORY AND PRACTICE IN FOREIGN TRADE

The Soviet Union, as said earlier, will not prove a sitting target for whatever designs the U. S. tries to execute through its trade policy. The Soviet Union will be a moving target, and a moving target that seeks not alone to dodge and parry, but aims at achieving ends of its own. As the United States tries through trade to produce results it wants, Moscow will do all it can not only to negate U. S. efforts, but to turn those efforts against the U. S. itself, and to otherwise use trade relationships in its continuing struggle against the United States. This, we can safely assume, will be true regardless of what the U. S. does, be it to continue trade denial as is, to refine the trade denial system to make it more effective, to drop denial and resort to trade promotion in the hope of bridging the hostility between systems, or to use trade in a contest of maneuver.

Chapter Nineteen

FOR THE SOVIETS: FOREIGN TRADE AN IDEAL INSTRUMENT OF REVOLUTIONARY STRUGGLE

The Soviet leaders, in a tradition that has held up from the earliest days of Lenin, look upon foreign trade as peculiarly well suited to the furtherance of world revolutionary purposes. If their words and deeds can be taken as a guide, which in this case they surely can, the Soviet leaders are convinced that in the area of trade are to be found, on the one hand, one of the major vulnerabilities of the capitalist world, and, on the other, one of the most effective means they themselves can bring to bear in positive ways in their unceasing efforts to achieve that final world victory to which they are so deeply committed.

Theory Translated Into Action

Faith in the efficacy of trade and trade policy as an instrument of warfare against the capitalist enemy has been the source of many of the most important and far-reaching of Soviet strategic decisions, and these include decisions of Lenin, Stalin, and Khrushchev. Lenin staked heavily, and it turned out successfully, on the belief that the hungry urge of Western capitalists to regain a foothold in the Russian market offered a sure means for turning away the hostility of the capitalist world and securing for the new Soviet Republic a sorely needed economic and political breathing spell. He moved with equal assurance to capitalize on his theory that greed for trade would drive individual capitalists and capitalist countries to do anything, ranging from helping the Soviets to build the strength necessary to do capitalism in, to rending and tearing each other in the fratricidal struggles that would be a necessary prelude to capitalism's final destruction. Stalin based much of his postwar strategy (for example the "struggle" against the Marshall Plan and the "division of the world into two hostile camps") on the concept that dependence on markets and trade constitutes a vital weakness of capitalist countries, while the same concept led Khrushchev to launch the great Soviet drive to woo and win or, lacking that, to subvert and win, the newly emerging and the developing countries of the world.

The conviction so manifestly held by Lenin and his successors that foreign trade, like history, can be made to work for the Soviet Union and its world revolutionary cause derives from: (1) the hard fact that total control of foreign trade within the Soviet Union has always been vested in their hands as masters of the USSR; and (2) the theoretical concept that an ever-expanding foreign trade is a life and death necessity for survival of the capitalist order.

Chapter Twenty

BASIS FOR CONFIDENCE: FOREIGN TRADE A PLIABLE INSTRUMENT OF POLICY

The establishment of a "state monopoly of foreign trade," in all of its phases and aspects, was one of the first steps taken by the Bolshevik regime to implement its program of "socializing" the Russian economy. The effect of this step was to make the foreign trade of the USSR an instrument of power of the ruling regime. And this it has since remained. As an instrument of power, foreign trade has been, and is, wielded and manipulated like other instruments of power, including the armed forces, the party itself, the thought control system, the secret police, etc., in the interest of attaining the basic political aims and objectives of the regime, both at home and abroad.

How the Instrument Is Used

Some of the aims and objectives on which foreign trade has important bearing have been constant, with the result that related foreign trade policies have also been constant. Thus, throughout Soviet history the Soviet rulers have attached high priority to self-sufficiency. Foreign trade policy has consequently been tailored to this autarkic purpose. With but one major exception in Soviet history, resources of the Soviet Union have never been used in substantial quantities for the purchase abroad of articles of general consumption. This one exception, of course, was the wheat deals of 1963-64 which required the outlay of some $800 million of Soviet holdings of gold and hard currencies. Imports of the USSR have centered almost exclusively on goods required for the expansion of the Soviet economic and military power base. Whether under a Stalin, a Khrushchev, or a whoever, the Soviet trading authorities have left no stones unturned to get from abroad items required to meet heavy industry and military development plans. And they have not hesitated to turn their backs on the best of bargains—sometimes even near gifts —when a significant connection with development operations of this type was lacking.

Other of the Soviet aims and objectives with which foreign trade is related are subject to shifting priorities. Needless to say, the conduct of foreign trade in these cases shifts accordingly. Thus, at times, expansion of a given sector of the economy takes precedence over all else. In this case, foreign trade activities are channeled in directions that will maximize support for the priority goals necessary, without regard to costs or other considerations that govern the conduct of foreign trade in nontotalitarian states. In the 1928-31 period, Soviet traders raked up virtually everything in the Soviet Union that was saleable abroad, including vast quantities of wheat and other grains that alone stood between millions and certain starvation, in order to buy abroad on the best terms they could the goods required for forced-draft industrialization and mechanized collectivization. In 1938-39, when the cherished expansion of the industrial base of the country was suddenly subordinated to a build-up of the immediate military readiness of the country, foreign trade operations were redirected accordingly. And so it was in 1957-58 when Khrushchev and his associates took the decision to accelerate realization of goals set under the seven-year plan.

At other times, strictly political considerations have been given overriding priority in the determination of policies in the foreign trade field. In 1932, Stalin's desire to intensify the great depression raging in the West was an important factor in the abrupt and precipitous drop in

Soviet purchases abroad, at very great costs to the industrial development that had previously overridden everything else. Again, critical need of the Soviet Union for Western supplies during the years immediately following World War II did not deter Stalin from holding purchases of such supplies to an absolute minimum in the belief that this would generate important pressures on, if not a degenerative process within, the United States. And to cite some minor but still significant instances: the Soviet Union, for strictly political reasons, in 1949 ended purchases of wool from Australia despite its own pressing need for such wool; threatened in 1958 to halt a trade with Finland that worked strongly to its own advantage; and in 1949 cut off a major source of badly needed dollars by abruptly halting chrome and manganese sales to the United States. On a different front, all trade with Yugoslavia, from which the USSR benefited far more than Yugoslavia, was embargoed for political reasons beginning in 1948, and an abrupt change in trade and other economic relations with Communist China and Albania carried out in 1960.

Given their power to manipulate foreign trade at will—to speed it up or slow it down; to cut it off or to redirect it by country or area or product; to live without it or to give it highest priority, the Soviet leaders quite naturally feel great assurance with regard to their ability to outdo their capitalist adversaries—who have no such freedom of action—in any game of using trade in the continuing struggle for world supremacy.

Chapter Twenty-One

BASIS FOR CONFIDENCE: FOREIGN MARKETS AND THE "LAWS" GOVERNING CAPITALISM

This confidence is all the greater because of the theoretical dictum, which has the force in Soviet thinking of an immutable law of history, that capitalist countries must expand their foreign trade or perish. This dictum was born of Lenin's study of "imperialism" or better his digest of the studies of imperialism by others. Lenin convinced himself that the natural evolution of capitalism had brought it to the stage of "monopoly capitalism," where it is completely dependent for survival on its ability to find ever new and greater foreign markets for the disposal of its inevitably mounting surpluses of both products and capital. Lacking such foreign markets, he believed, capitalism, both generically and in particular countries, would choke to death on those growing surpluses.

64

The dictum has been, and continues to be, the basis of an operational faith on the part of the Soviet leaders that foreign trade manipulation can be used in several major ways to weaken and otherwise to hasten the destruction of the capitalist world.

1. *The Withdrawal of Markets from Capitalist Exploitation*

Once it became clear that revolution was not to spread from Russia to the advanced countries of the West, Lenin's strategy for achieving world revolution was founded principally on the calculation that if, at the very moment that capitalism needed greater and greater markets, the areas open to capitalist exploitation were systematically reduced, there would take place a corresponding magnification and intensification of the "contradictions" which he believed are irrepressibly operating within the capitalist world and are relentlessly preparing for the demise of the capitalist order.

How Lenin Saw the Matter: Lenin did not himself attempt to utilize this powerful weapon that presumably his control of the vast reaches of Russia placed in his hands. He apparently toyed with the idea for a while after first seizing power, but evidently gave up any thoughts in that direction when it became clear that the Soviet Union needed economic support from the West far more than the western capitalists needed Soviet markets. However, Lenin still argued that the road to victory lay not through a direct onslaught on capitalism in the leading industrialized countries, but through the revolutionary capture and withdrawal from capitalist exploitation of one after another of the colonial or "imperialist dominated" areas of Asia, Africa and South America. Once a sufficient number of these "exploited areas" were in fact withdrawn from capitalism's domain, the capitalist, or as Lenin would say "imperialist," countries would be forced back onto themselves and subjected to a deepening internal crisis that would either bring about the collapse of the established order, or so weaken capitalist forces that their ultimate defeat would be relatively easy to bring about.

A Major Determinant of Stalin's Policies: Stalin not only accepted Lenin's thinking regarding the strategic possibilities of "trade withdrawal" but made it very much his own. He refined Lenin's rather loose generalizations into a body of doctrines having to do with this and related matters. He himself had a go at a withdrawal operation in the early 1930s when he thought to intensify what he considered the "general crisis of capitalism" that was manifesting itself in the great depression. Like Lenin, however, he came to recognize that the importance of the Soviet market alone was not sufficient to produce a decisive impact on the capitalist world. Moreover, he too came very much to want assistance from the capitalist world to build up his own strength in the face of the growing danger from Hitler.

After the war, however, when the vast region extending from Albania through China, from the Adriatic Sea to the Sea of Japan, with its "one-third of mankind," came under effective Soviet control, Stalin believed he was in a position to wreak havoc on capitalism by closing his immense empire to capitalist trade, particularly to trade on the part of the United States. First belabored by Zdanov as the Soviet theoretical rationale for rejecting the participation of the East European countries in the Marshall Plan, and for calling on communists in Western Europe to frustrate execution of the Plan there, the key role that withdrawal could play in the future course of the "world revolutionary struggle" was detailed by Stalin in an article published in October, 1952, entitled "The Economic Problems of Socialism in the USSR." Asserting that "the most important economic consequence of the second World War must be considered the disintegration of a single, all-embracing world market . . . and its replacement by two parallel markets opposing each other," Stalin went on to argue:

> "This means that the sphere of operation of the main capitalist powers —the United States, Britain and France—will not continue to grow but will be reduced, that the conditions of the world market for these countries will deteriorate, and that the number of idle enterprises will grow. The above is in fact the essence of the deepening general crisis of the world capitalist system connected with the disintegration of the world market. The above is felt by the capitalists themselves as it would be rather difficult not to feel the loss of such markets as the USSR and China. They have tried to overcome the above difficulties with the help of the Marshall Plan, the war in Korea, the arms race and the militarization of industry. This solution reminds one of the saying about the drowning man who clutches at straws."

Stalin came as close to enforcing economic isolation on his captive socialist camp as he possibly could, except that he saw it as enforcing isolation on the capitalist world. Trade patterns that had existed for generations before World War II were turned upside down. Everything was done that could be done to insure that capitalism would in fact be forced "to choke on its surpluses." And the withdrawal effort was hammered through despite its costs for the USSR and the other communist countries, which we now know to have been very great. Stalin's empire and its "heartland," the USSR itself, were at the time of Stalin's death in 1953 beset by an accumulation of ills and problems that extended into every corner of the economy. And while many factors were responsible, certainly among the most important was Stalin's go at economic warfare between "systems."

Carry Over to the Present: Stalin's successors were acutely aware of the costs engendered by the withdrawal operation. Yet for several years they stubbornly stuck to it. Only in the second half of the 1950s did they back down and move for a renewal of significant trade contacts with the industrialized countries of the West. And when the break came, it was not in terms of a change of heart or of a repudiation of a false doctrine, but a "retreat" of the order of Lenin's retreat on the occasion of adopting the New Economic Policy in 1921 and Stalin's "united front" against Hitler in the mid-thirties. The underlying doctrinal concept was in no way questioned. Quite evidently the thought was merely to put it on ice for a later and more favorable day. Khrushchev continued to reaffirm the validity of the concept and used it to support his often repeated boast that the "balance of world forces" had irrevocably shifted in favor of the communist cause. Moreover, and more important, the concept was admittedly the source of the Soviet decision reached in the mid-1950s and continued until now to seek to "liberate" through "trade and aid" and other devices the developing countries from the "new colonialist exploitation" of the United States and other western powers.

The *Party Program* that was adopted by the Communist Party of the Soviet Union at its Twenty-Second Congress in October, 1961, authoritatively reaffirmed the key place "market denial" continues to occupy in both Soviet strategy and Soviet expectations. This document, which was heralded as the "Communist Manifesto of the Twentieth Century," boldly asserted:

"Modern 'capitalism has made the *market problem* extremely acute. Imperialism is incapable of solving it, because lag of effective demand behind growth of production is one of its objective laws. Moreover, it retards the industrial development of the underdeveloped countries. The world capitalist market is shrinking relative to the more rapidly expanding production capacity. It is partitioned by countless customs barriers and restrictive fences and split into exclusive currency and finance zones. An acute competitive struggle for markets, spheres of investment, and sources of raw materials is under way in the imperialist camp. It is becoming doubly acute since the territorial sphere of capitalist domination has been greatly narrowed. . . .

"The break-away from capitalism of more and more countries; the weakening of imperialist positions in the economic competition with socialism; the break-up of the imperialist colonial system; the intensification of imperialist contradictions with the development of state-monopoly capitalism and the growth of militarism; the mounting internal instability and decay of the capitalist economy evidenced by the increasing inability of capitalism to make full use of the productive forces (low rates of production growth, periodic crisis, continuous undercapacity operation of production plant, and chronic unemployment); the mounting struggle between labor and capital; an acute intensification of contradictions within the world capitalist economy; an unprecedented growth of political reaction in all spheres, rejection of bourgeois freedoms and establishment of fascist and despotic regimes in a number of countries: and the profound crisis of bourgeois policy and ideology—all these are manifestations of the *general crisis of capitalism. . . .*

"Thus, *the world imperialism system is rent by deep-rooted and acute* contradictions. The antagonism of labour and capital, the contradictions between the people and the monopolies, growing militarism, the break-up of the colonial system, the contradictions between the imperialist countries, conflicts and contradictions between the young national states and the old colonial powers, and—most important of all—the rapid growth of world socialism, are sapping and destroying imperialism, leading to its weakening and collapse."

2. Readiness of Capitalists to Be Taken

With capitalists vitally dependent on foreign markets, they, according to the Leninist concept, can be depended upon to all but sell their souls to strike deals that promise to open new foreign trade and investment opportunities. Lenin set great store by this assumed inevitable characteristic. He relied upon it, as noted above, to enable the Soviet Union to ride the backs of its enemies out of the mire into which it had fallen during the first three years of Bolshevik power. Lenin is said to have joked that capitalists would cheerfully sell the rope with which they were to be hanged. Though possibly apocryphal, such a statement well summarizes Lenin's feelings about the matter.

Although less open about it, Stalin clearly shared Lenin's views. He quite evidently, for example, expected Americans after the war to go to all sorts of lengths in the way of price cutting, etc., to induce the Soviet Union to take off their hands surpluses of heavy equipment accumulated during the war, and to make purchases that would keep occupied the vastly expanded (in Stalin's view vastly overexpanded) U. S. industrial establishment. However, it was Khrushchev who seemed most taken up with this line of thinking. He constantly played the game of laying out "massive order" lures to various western governments, especially the U. S. (the 1958 "shopping list" letter to Eisenhower, to cite one example), to "capitalists" as a presumed entity, and to individual businessmen and firms. And he seemed genuinely surprised at failures of his targets to take the proffered bait.

3. Influencing Western Political Decisions

The Soviet leaders manifestly have a highly distorted view of how politics work in the United States and other capitalist countries, and

68

particularly of the decision-taking process. They conceive of a parallel in the capitalist countries to their own party-government arrangement. For the United States, they see a small group of "monopoly capitalists" (i.e. businessmen) consisting of the Rockefellers, the Du Ponts, the Mellons, the Fords, etc. as constituting a sort of U. S. version of the Presidium of the Central Committee of the Soviet Communist Party. In their minds this group, while having no official position, completely controls the governmental process. Operating from "Wall Street," it tells the President, the Congress, and any and everybody else what and what not to do. The group, so Soviet thinking goes, does not operate on its own but is responsible to the interests and demands of the American business community as a whole. Ergo, if the American business community can be brought "into deep involvement" in trade with the Soviet Union, a sure means is open for the Soviets to exercise an indirect but real influence on the formulation of any policies that might in one way or another jeopardize this trade. And the same general picture exists with regard to other major capitalist countries: For the British, it is "the City" that is all important; for the Germans, the Krupps and the heads of the other great cartels; and so on for the French, the Japanese and the Italians.

Cases in Point: Weird as this view may appear, the Soviets have on specific occasions energetically tried to use elements with important or potentially important trade ties with the USSR within these assumed "hidden governments" to secure governmental decisions favorable to themselves. In the case of the United States, for example, representatives of the Soviet government, extending finally up to Stalin himself, tried to involve the American business community in a pressure campaign to force a change in the decision to end the flow of Lend-Lease supplies to the USSR after the war. Also, Stalin and Khrushchev to an even greater extent tried on numerous occasions to arouse the ire of what they considered to be important representatives of the American business community against the U. S. restrictive policy, apparently in the genuine expectation that this could produce the results for which they hoped.

4. Generating Frictions

Leninist doctrine holds that one of the major "contradictions" (by a "contradiction" the communists mean a clash of interests) operating within the capitalist world is a "contradiction" between the major capitalist powers over the division of foreign markets. While a contradiction of this type is supposed to be made and kept operative by the workings of immutable historical forces, in this case as in so many others Leninism calls for helping history along. At the same time, in a situation of dangerous confrontation between the Soviet Union and its "socialist camp" on the one side, and the U. S. and "capitalist camp" on the other, the speed with which the contradiction produces significant results can be of decisive importance. Any divisive tendencies within capitalist ranks are consequently not just to be welcomed but assiduously promoted. To play upon the hunger of particular capitalist countries, or of particular elements within a single capitalist country, offers in the Soviet mind a sure means of adding force to divisive tendencies. This leads not only to a power advantage for the communist cause in the great conflict between systems, but it can also produce direct and immediate advantages for the USSR in the form of cut-throat competition between the western countries, and among individual western firms, for opportunities to serve the Soviet market.

Chapter Twenty-Two

A BIT OF PERTINENT HISTORY

The principles which form the basis of the Soviet strategy of using trade against the capitalist countries are, in a manner of speaking, not dissimilar from those that govern the practice of judo. The Soviets expect to capitalize on the very strengths of the capitalist countries and on the confidence and eagerness which those strengths generate. This can be well illustrated by a brief look at what happened between the United States and the USSR at the end of World War II.

Dreams of a Massive Postwar U.S.-Soviet Trade

One product of wartime cooperation between the United States and the USSR, particularly of the "trade" relationships developed under Lend-Lease, was widespread excitement within the United States with regard to the possibility of large-scale postwar trade between the two countries. Both within and outside the government, massive preparatory work was done in anticipation of this trade. It was widely estimated that Soviet requirements to meet reconstruction needs and to resume and catch up on war-interrupted development, which now assuredly would be in the direction of an overall improvement in the economic life of the country, would be in the range of several billion dollars a year for a period of fifteen or so years. No one expected the Soviet Union to be able to operate on a pay-as-you-go basis in meeting these requirements; planning was almost exclusively in terms of long-term credit financing.

The excitement and planning within American circles was inevitably

70

transmitted to Russian representatives, including those at the highest levels. And concrete suggestions were passed to Soviet authorities, frequently by high U. S. officials on an "unofficial" basis, that a request for a very large trade loan should be prepared for submission before or just after the war's end. The loan figure most often bruited around was $5 billion for a starter, but many Americans thought in even more expansive terms. For example, a proposal was seriously brought forward by a group of U. S. government and industry leaders for a U. S. loan of several billion dollars to finance Soviet procurement in the U. S. of railway rolling stock alone.

Soviet Foot Dragging

While individual Soviet representatives at the "working level" often shared the American enthusiasm, there was a marked lack of official Soviet responsiveness. While far-ranging shopping lists for materials and equipment to meet postwar needs were submitted through official channels, they were within the context of the Lend-Lease Protocol agreement—that is, for consideration as part of the U.S. Lend-Lease program. Meanwhile, the Soviet government dragged its feet on the one concrete postwar credit proposal that was officially before it.

As a means of winding up Lend-Lease transactions in an orderly manner under terms of the Lend-Lease law, the U. S. proposed, in the fourth of its wartime supply protocols, that the USSR agree to assume financial responsibility for nonmilitary manufactures ordered to special Soviet specifications under Lend-Lease that would remain undelivered (i.e. in the "pipeline") at the war's end. Otherwise, the Lend-Lease law would require cancellation of the orders, a step that would entail financial loss to the U. S. government, and presumably ultimately also to the Soviet government; produce disruptive effects on the American manufacturers involved; and, most important from the Soviet standpoint, deny the Soviets benefit of the products, virtually all of which were clearly intended to meet high-priority reconstruction and developmental needs. The U. S. offered the USSR a long-term loan of $300 million at a modest interest rate to enable it to cover the orders.

Moscow interposed innumerable objections to that arrangement and stubbornly refused to accept it. One factor motivating the Soviets, and this was clear at the time, was their belief that the United States would face a crisis of overproduction after the war, and that it would be only a matter of time before not only machinery and equipment then being produced for the Soviet Union, but also almost anything else that the Soviets might wish to buy, could be procured at a fraction of the price that prevailed at the war's end. Later, however, the evidence indicates that a second and more decisive factor was also at work, and in this factor also seems to lie the explanation for the ambivalence of the Kremlin regarding postwar U. S. loans in general: Stalin was debating whether, given a postwar economic crisis in the United States on the scale he anticipated, it would be in the Soviet interest to take the United States off the overproduction hook almost regardless of the liberality of the conditions the U. S. might offer.

The Loan Request Puzzle

At the beginning of January, 1945, a puzzling and still unexplained twist took place. The Soviet Foreign Ministry notified the U. S. Embassy in Moscow that the Soviet government had decided to "accede to U. S. wishes" and to accept a U. S. loan in the amount of $6 billion to finance postwar purchases in the United States. No official U. S. reply was made to this communication, although Soviet authorities were informally told that the United States could not consider a regular postwar loan unless and until the Soviet government had made a positive response to the proposal for the $300 million Lend-Lease pipeline arrangement.

The Soviet government did not follow up in any way. At the Potsdam meeting in August, 1945, Stalin made no reference to the Soviet loan "request" or to any other aspect of trade matters. Early in 1946, the Soviet Embassy in Washington submitted a query to the Lend-Lease Administrator as to the possibility of a $1 billion loan, without any reference to the earlier $6 billion request. Again the United States made no official response, but informally the point was repeated that the $300 million pipeline matter had first to be disposed of. In this case also there was no Soviet follow-up. Only in April, 1947, on the occasion of Stalin's meeting with General Marshall in Moscow, was the matter of the Soviet requests brought up by the Soviets. Even then, Stalin made no effort to secure a substantive discussion of the possibilities of a U. S. loan, but simply used the matter to counter General Marshall's complaints regarding Soviet conduct.

Meanwhile, the Soviets had gone along with the $300 million pipeline agreement, but only after it had become clear that machinery and equipment, including a number of complete plants which they had been heavily counting on, were in process of being finally lost to them.

Soviets Initiate "Trade Denial"

Aside from this one step, Moscow did nothing to build upon the trade relationships that had been established during the war. Instead, the USSR

72

showed an increasingly marked loss of interest in the American market. And this was at a time when materials and equipment of the type needed and desired by the USSR had not yet come into tight supply and their price remained fairly reasonable. Moreover, none of the U. S. restrictive measures, on which the Soviets were later to place such emphasis, had yet been brought into force by the United States. The whole restrictive system, in fact, was more than a year away. Also the general climate prevailing in the U. S. in regard to trade transactions with the USSR remained quite good. Yet Soviet purchases in the U. S. in 1948 fell to less than $28 million, one of the lowest figures since recognition in 1934. And this on the morrow, as it were, of a four-year period extending from 1942 through 1945 during which the USSR received from the United States successive annual shipments of $1.4 billion, $3.0 billion, $3.5 billion, and $1.8 billion.

Chapter Twenty-Three

MEANING OF SOVIET THEORIES AND PRACTICES FOR THE U. S.

What in practical terms is the significance of Soviet theories and practices with respect to foreign trade?

The answer to this question requires repetition of points made earlier. Yet for convenience it is probably well to present them once again in summary form. The general answer falls into two parts.

Basic Implications

First, for the Soviets, foreign trade takes place only by sufferance of the ruling authorities; its course is not the product of spontaneously operating economic factors, but of conscious political policy; decisions as to when, where, how and with whom foreign trade is carried on are arrived at on the basis of considerations that are independent of, and often counter to, the requirements and needs of foreign trade itself. A foreign trade policy as such does not and cannot exist; foreign trade is an instrument of policy and not an object of policy; it is a phase, a facet, of a total of activities designed to achieve the basic objectives of the Soviet regime; it is an integral of the Marxist-Leninist system that exists in the USSR and is inseparable from other elements in that system.

Second, for noncommunist nations that trade with the Soviets, trade with the USSR must be approached with an awareness that trade relations with the USSR cannot be divorced from other relations; that the sole purpose of the Soviets in engaging in trade is in one way or another to further their aim of destroying those with whom they are trading; and that the very fact that the Soviets are engaging in a particular trade at a particular time reflects the importance the trade has for Soviet purposes.

Regarding Specifics

Particular points that need to be noted within the context of this general answer are:

1. *Limited Trade*: Soviet theories and practices regarding foreign trade with noncommunists make large scale trade between East and West highly unlikely, particularly trade between the United States and the USSR as a regular thing. In other words, as long as those policies and practices persist, trade will be far under what it would be were the "economics of trade" allowed free play. The only circumstances under which trade between the U. S. and the USSR is likely to obtain a substantial magnitude, and then only for a temporary period, are: (a) where the USSR for political reasons has extraordinary needs, as, for example, has been the case over the past few years in consequence of the Khrushchev decision for a forced-draft build-up of neglected areas of the Soviet industrial plant, and as was the case with the 1963-64 Soviet wheat shortage; (b) where Soviet purchases would be subsidized by the U. S. through uneconomic credit terms, or below cost pricing; or (c) the USSR finds itself with windfall surpluses, for example in consequence of a succession of unusually good harvests or unusual imbalances in production against plan, which would enable it to earn unusual amounts of foreign exchange.

2. *Economic Advantage to the Soviets*: The Soviet policies and practices insure that in trade relations with a state, be it the United States or some other state, *which does not maintain political control over its trade,* the greater *economic* benefits will accrue to the USSR. The statement is often made that in foreign trade, as in any other form of trade, both sides benefit, since otherwise there would be no trade. This, it would seem, is true almost by definition. But it does not follow that both sides necessarily benefit equally. In strictly economic terms, the Soviets need trade with the United States far more than the United States needs trade with them; what the Soviets get helps them far more. But beyond this, given full political control on the Soviet side and less than that on the other side, the Soviets are in the driver's seat. It is theirs to pick and choose, to move levels up and down, to bide for time or to move suddenly to take advantage of an opportunity, to play

74

off one competitor against another. It is theirs to limit deals to bargains from the standpoint of worth to them of what they get as against the worth of what they give up. It is theirs to set the tempo so as best to meet their own developmental needs. It is theirs to create dependencies while leaving their own hands free.

3. *Political Advantage to the Soviets*: Trade with a state that does not maintain political control is certain also to redound to the *political* benefit of the USSR. Under the Soviet system, all trade is directed toward serving national ends. Unless imports from abroad are necessary to meet a requirement set by the government through its planning apparatus, the communists do not buy. And insofar as advanced Western countries are concerned, particularly the United States, the Soviets do not sell except as necessary to buy. Against this, the direct aim of trade in the case of a free economy, such as exists in the United States, is normally to benefit the individual or firm engaging in the trade. National benefit may or may not follow, depending on chance or the working of economic laws, for it does not enter into the calculus of the individual western trader. Under the established rules of the game, he buys or sells according to whether he can make profit. He relies upon his government to take care of national interests when and as necessary through restraints and controls. In the absence of these, his guide is the workings of the market place.*

4. *Dichotomy of Purposes*: The complexity of the problem raised by Soviet trade theories and practices is not limited to the simple matter of a state trading system vs. a private system. There is a much deeper, more fundamental purpose. The communist trading system is part of a larger system that views as its major mission the replacement of the capitalist order by a socialist order. There is thus an inescapable dichotomy between international trade as practiced by the capitalist West, particularly by the United States, and international trade as practiced by the communists, particularly the USSR, which is anticapitalist in nature and purpose. This dichotomy obviously does not preclude extensive trade between communists and capitalists. But it does preclude

---

* It is important here to note that bilateral trade agreements such as are entered into by many western countries with the USSR do not materially alter the "national interest vs individual interest" characteristic of Soviet-Western trade, as those agreements do not involve commitments to buy and sell on either side. They only set permissive limits, or levels of intent, for trade in various categories of goods. It is left to regular trade agencies (that is state on the Soviet side and private on the western) to work out the nature, scope, and conditions of actual trade within the broad framework provided by the agreements.

a type of trade relationship between the two comparable to the relationship that exists among western states.

5. *No Automatic Bridge Building*: In this connection, it is frequently assumed that certain economic and political consequences will more or less automatically flow from a substantial increase in trade between the United States and the USSR in the way of increased understanding between governments, more extensive contacts between peoples, growing interdependence, a changing pattern of industrial production on the communist side, a relaxation of tensions, growing cooperation in international affairs, etc. Given, however, the Soviet system and the purposes to which it is committed, and given the extent to which foreign trade is subordinated to this system and its purposes, consequences such as these can hardly follow no matter what the amount of trade. With the Soviets, trade does not shape politics but politics trade. Instead of being a means of bridging the gap between systems, trade in Soviet hands is made to serve conflict, not cooperation, between systems.

During the war, great store was placed by many thoughtful Americans on the beneficial results that would surely flow from the massive trade exchanges and contacts that were taking place between the United States and the USSR under Lend-Lease. What happened to those hopes and expectations? In the brief span of four years, from the U. S. to the USSR flowed just under $10 billion of goods of almost every description, and of importance to every strata of Soviet life, touching and affecting nearly every element of the Soviet population. Literally tens of thousands of persons on both sides engaged in the managing and handling of this flow of goods. Yet no discernible impact on the Soviet system, Soviet attitudes, or Soviet policies was produced by the trade and contacts. Even while the trade was at its height, the Soviets appeared immune to the influences trade is assumed to exercise. And while hundreds of millions of dollars of American goods still remained in warehouses and at staging depots or were stacked in crates at ports and in railway yards in the Soviet Union, the Kremlin launched its cold war campaign against the United States—against those elements in and characteristics of the American system that had made possible the production of goods that still were overflowing the Soviet Union, and had led to the policies that caused those billions of dollars of other goods to be marshaled in support of the Soviet Union.

PART 5

AN ESSENTIAL BACKGROUND FACTOR: THE SOVIETS AND "ECONOMIC COMPETITION BETWEEN SYSTEMS"

Chapter Twenty-Four

ECONOMIC COMPETITION AND THE WORLD STRUGGLE

Nothing could be more vain, nor more dangerous, than to single out one or another of the varied threats the Soviet Union mounts against the U. S. as the most important or the most serious. The Soviet attack is all-encompassing. It ranges from an arms race to an ideological struggle for men's minds. It involves blandishments and threats; bargaining and blackmail; diplomatic maneuvering and crisis mongering; the soft touch and the blunt blow; commitments and betrayals. It is direct and indirect; frontal and oblique; open and clandestine. It poses at one and the same time a military challenge that could lead to a thermonuclear war by either accident or design, or to a local clash with all its risks of escalation; a challenge of conquest by indirection through so-called "wars of liberation"; a challenge of the sudden-sprung crisis; a challenge of penetration and subversion; a propaganda challenge; an economic challenge.

Varied and Interchangeable "Forms of Struggle"

We cannot afford to focus on one or more of the Soviet challenges to the exclusion of the others. We cannot afford, for example, to concentrate with a singleness of purpose on the contest for influence over the developing countries, lest we find ourselves confronted with missiles in a Cuba, or in the midst of an acute crisis over a Berlin. We cannot, above all else, assume that the Soviets will do "this," while they will surely not do "that." We cannot gamble that the conflict in which they are engaging us will involve only certain sorts of tests. We can perhaps calculate that at a particular period of time and under a particular set of circumstances the Soviets will pursue one line of endeavor while avoid-

77

ing for the moment another. But we cannot calculate that, as a matter of general principle, Soviet methods will encompass this and not something else; if we do we shall risk getting caught seriously short. The communists themselves have spelled all of this out quite clearly and frankly on any number of occasions, most recently in the 1961 Party Program where it was explained.

> "The success of the struggle . . . for the victory of the revolution will depend upon how well the working class and the Party master the use of all forms of struggle . . . how well they are prepared for any swift and sudden replacement of one form of struggle by another form of struggle."

Economic Competition a Heavily Stressed Form of Struggle

It is in this context that we must view the heavy, and sometimes overriding, emphasis the Soviets place on "economic competition between systems." Soviet leaders have often asserted that the victory they expect to win will be won through a demonstration of the "economic superiority" of their system. This was a some-time theme of Lenin, at least after the shattering of his dreams for a quick spread of violent revolution over Europe; of Stalin, when he was not in unguarded moments speaking of a more direct approach; and of Khrushchev. With Khrushchev the theme took on the tone of a conviction; at least it was almost a constant. He repeatedly argued that an ultimate Soviet triumph on a world scale was assured by the "superiority" of the Soviet economic system; that the Soviets would demonstrate to all the peoples of the world that the way to economic strength, the way to economic well-being for the people is through a socialist economy. And, reflecting Khrushchev, the theme pervaded the Party Program of 1961, the closing paragraphs of which asserted:

> "The achievement of communism in the USSR will be the greatest victory mankind has ever won throughout its long history. Every new step made towards the bright peaks of communism inspires the working masses in all countries, renders immense moral support to the struggle for the liberation of all peoples from social and national oppression, and brings closer the triumph of Marxism-Leninism on a world-wide scale.

> "When the Soviet people will enjoy the blessings of communism, new hundreds of millions of people on earth will say: 'we are for communism.' It is not through war with other countries, but by the example of a more perfect organization of society, by rapid progress in developing the productive forces, the creation of all conditions for the happiness and well-being of man, that the ideas of communism win the minds and hearts of the masses."

Meanwhile, of course, the Soviets have given anything but convincing evidence that they are in truth relying solely or even principally on an "economic competition between systems" to achieve victory. As Stalin talked about economic competition, he spoke also of war as the indispensable midwife of revolution, and he planned and acted more in accordance with the latter than the former. Khrushchev on the morrow of the adoption of the new Party Program with its emphasis on peaceful competition risked nuclear war in an attempt to plant missiles in Cuba. And Soviet economic management and planning—the all-important resources allocation pattern—continue directed not toward the building of a society of "plenty," about which so much lip service is given, but toward the further and relentless strengthening of the sinews of Soviet power.

However, to say that we cannot sit back and depend upon the Soviets to confine their conflict with us to the economic sphere in no way implies that economic competition is not of major importance in the conflict. The point is that while the Soviets do not put all of their eggs in one basket, each of the baskets is of great moment to them. While not neglecting "other forms of struggle," they unquestionably have high hopes of obtaining significant advantage over the United States through economic competition. The whole body of their doctrine teaches that through "scientific" planning and "scientific" management a "socialist" system must necessarily produce results vastly superior to those obtainable under an "anarchistic" capitalistic system. "In contrast to capitalism," the 1961 Program asserts, "the planned socialist system of economy combines accelerated technical progress with the full employment of all able-bodied citizens."

The economic avenue, moreover, may have become far more attractive to the Soviet leaders as other avenues have been narrowed or made too risky by world developments. It may be, in fact, that despite continued efforts along other lines, and a continued readiness to employ other means, the Soviet leaders have come to suspect in the back of their minds that if they cannot achieve their triumph through economic competition they are unlikely to achieve it at all. And, of course, keeping up in the economic race is of decisive importance with regard to maintaining a capability to keep up in the other crucial contests in which the regime is engaged, the capability to keep pace in the armaments race, in the space race, in the competition for influence in the developing areas of the world, in the ideological competition, and in the contest for preeminent world prestige.

Dual Nature of Economic Competition

There are two main aspects of the "economic competition between systems" as the Soviets have spelled it out. One is on the home front: it centers on the building of the most productive society; the attainment of the most rapid rate of growth; the achievement of scientific and technological preeminence. The other is a direct competition in the developing areas of the world. This has to do with "trade and aid"; with the extension of technical assistance; with the determination of the path which an emerging society shall take, whether toward "capitalism" or "socialism."

Chapter Twenty-Five

BASIC GOAL: TO PROVE THE ECONOMIC SUPERIORITY OF THE SOVIET SYSTEM

The 1961 *Party Program* boasted:

"In the current decade (1961-70) the Soviet Union ... will surpass the strongest and richest capitalist country, the U.S.A., in production per head of population; the people's standard of living and their cultural and technical standards will improve substantially; everyone will live in easy circumstances; all collective and state farms will become highly productive and profitable enterprises; the demand of the Soviet people for well appointed housing will, in the main, be satisfied; hard physical work will disappear; the USSR will have the shortest working day. . . .

"The material and technical basis for communism will be built up by the end of the second decade (1971-80) insuring an abundance of material and cultural values for the whole population. . . . This means complete electrification of the country and perfection on this basis of the techniques, technologies, and organization of social production in all the fields of the national economy; comprehensive mechanization of production operations and a growing degree of their automation; widespread use of chemistry in the national economy; vigorous development of new, economically effective branches of production, new types of power and new material; all-round and rational utilization of natural, material and labor resources; organic fusion of science and production, and rapid scientific and technical progress; a high cultural and technical level for the working people; and substantial superiority over the more developed capitalist countries in productivity of labor, which constitutes the most important prerequisite for the victory of the communist system. As a result, the USSR will possess productive forces of unparalleled might; it will surpass the technical level of the most developed countries and occupy first place in the world in per capita production."

Claims From the Past

The projection of a future in which the Soviet Union shall stand

80

economically supreme and with all the world literally at its feet is not a new phenomenon. It has been an article of faith of the Soviet leadership since the establishment of the Bolshevik regime that the Soviet system provides a sure means of finally overcoming all of the problems of production; that it is inherently superior to the capitalist system; and that it is only a matter of time before it will enable the Soviets to surpass all rivals, especially the United States, not only in production (including per capita production), but in the effective utilization of production. Stalin as early as January, 1933, said on occasion of the announced completion of the first five-year plan, apparently with some conviction:

> "The results of the five year plan have shown that the capitalist system of economy is bankrupt and unstable; that it has become obsolete and must give way to another, a higher, Soviet, socialist system of economy; that the only system of economy that has no fear of crises and is able to overcome the difficulties which capitalism cannot solve is the Soviet system of economy."

The uncovering of some serious deficiencies in Soviet accomplishments (in 1941 actual Soviet production for most industrial sectors was still appreciably under what it was supposed to have been at the end of 1932), plus a closer wartime acquaintanceship with U. S. productive power, brought Stalin to a more sober estimate of possibilities. In his later years he spoke of "catching up" with the United States somewhere in the mid-1960s in absolute (not per capita) production and only in heavy industry categories. (The figures he used, moreover, were those of U. S. production in 1939-40; not a projection of 1965 ff.) After Stalin, however, and particularly following Sputnik, the leadership revived its enthusiastic optimism. Khrushchev announced and then exulted over plans to surpass the U. S. in various categories of production in per capita terms within a specified and astonishingly short span of years. He evidently convinced himself and others that the first break would come in the "per capita production of meat, butter and milk," within "two or three years" from 1959.

How the Contest Shapes Up

We can take considerable satisfaction that Khrushchev's predictions of the 1950s have turned out as faulty as Stalin's of the 1930s. And we would have every reason to view the future with calm if the Soviets should in fact concentrate their major "competitive" efforts, as they claim to intend to concentrate them, on matching the U. S. in across-the-board economic development—that is, in a broad-ranged advance encompassing all sectors of the economy, including the consumer sectors. For in such an across-the-board competition the U. S. would have little

81

to worry about. We should have no difficulty in keeping well ahead throughout the foreseeable future in terms of both overall production and productivity. So far, while the percentage gap between Soviet production and U. S. production has steadily narrowed, the absolute gap has widened with equal steadiness. Where U. S. gross national product exceeded the Soviet some years ago by only a hundred and fifty billion dollars, the excess is now well over three hundred billion. And within the next eight or ten years it will probably approach five hundred billion, without taking account of the decline in the Soviet rate of growth that has become so marked in the past four years. Unless we do something to ourselves, the U. S. should achieve a smashing success in a *general* economic competition with the USSR, whether measurement is in terms of GNP, per capita production, labor productivity, the well-being of the populace, or simply general affluence.

How the USSR May Gain Advantage

What we have to face up to, and what we need to be concerned about, is the very likely possibility that the Soviets do not have in mind, and will not attempt to engage us in, a *general* economic competition at all. Of course they talk in terms of this sort of competition. And it is possible that they have a vague intention of someday seriously embarking on the program—which for the Soviets would have to be truly revolutionary—necessary to outdo the United States in the building of a society of plenty. Up to now, however, they have limited themselves to a far more restricted operation. They have concentrated on a competition to surpass the United States only in those phases of production, in those areas of economic capability, that have to do with national power and the base on which national power rests.

A Drive for Technological Preeminence?

What the Soviets appear to be up to is not to surpass the U. S. in over-all production, particularly not to surpass it in general affluence. Its aim appears to be the attainment of technological preeminence over the United States. This is how we should read the challenge of "economic competition between systems." And in making this reading and weighing its implications, here are some basic points we need to keep in mind:

1. The domestic and foreign goals the Soviet regime has set for itself and the timetable it has established for the realization of these goals are completely unrealistic in terms of the present or potential capabilities of Russia and the Russian people. The regime, in addition

to trying to make over the country internally, has taken on the whole world, as it were, while the Soviet Union is still a second-class power in many respects when compared to the United States, not to speak of the industrialized West as a whole.

2.   The regime has sought to succeed in its ambitious schemes not by building up Soviet resources and strength across-the-board (that is by going through a broad development process comparable to the one the United States, Britain, Germany, and Japan went through), but by pushing far ahead in a selected power sector and then utilizing this advance as a springboard for a quantum jump in its overall power position.

3.   Thus Stalin determined (with considerable success) to move Russia from a position of a weakling among modern nations to a great power status through forced-draft development of heavy industry (backed up by collectivized agriculture). He paid not the slightest attention to the glaring weaknesses of the Soviet economy in virtually every field other than heavy industry. He even quite deliberately followed policies that intensified those weaknesses. His goal was to push far forward in this one field and to use achievements in it as a platform for effecting a leap to a new power plateau.

4.   After the war, Stalin (and his successors) followed the same course, combining a drive forward in weapons modernization and the development of a nuclear capability with a renewed and intensified drive in the heavy industry sector (the power base sector), again disregarding the need for balanced development.

5.   In recent years—that is, since their initial startling successes in rocketry and space exploration—the Soviets have evidently focused on advanced technology as the most promising means of achieving another quantum jump, with space and related activities serving as a focal point of their hopes and efforts.

6.   The Soviet goal is not confined to winning any specific competition, in space or otherwise. The aim is leadership—preeminence—in all major scientific and technological fields. The regime has made it a matter of national policy to strive with every possible means for such preeminence. The leaders, in other words, have shown an acute awareness of the importance of the "balance of technological power" and are trying by every means to tip it in their favor. As a measure of their intention:

—As early as February 8, 1958 Khrushchev had stated: "Soviet science and our higher educational establishments must always hold first place in the world. It is a matter of honor for the Soviet scientists to hold the leading place in all branches of knowledge."

—In April, 1961 a Party-government decision on the reorganization of Soviet scientific research directed the scientific community to seek the earliest possible primacy for the Soviet Union "in all basic directions."

—In June, 1961 a Party-government message of greeting to a meeting of two thousand members of the Soviet scientific elite in the Kremlin again declared that "soviet science and technology must take leading positions in the world in all basic directions at the earliest possible date." The message noted the high priority given to science in state planning: "In socialist society, the development of science for the first time in history has been raised to the level of the most important task of the state."

—On November 6, 1964, several weeks after Khrushchev's ouster, Party First Secretary Breshnev said at the Kremlin Palace: ". . . . On the basis of the union of science and the latest technology, the Soviet Union is advancing confidently into a leading position in key areas of world scientific and technical progress. In our country, this is of *decisive* importance."

Inferiority Coupled with Confidence

The Soviets quite evidently have a very high regard for U. S. technological competence. In fact they openly acknowledge that in many areas the U. S. has a strong lead over the USSR, and scientists and technologists have been officially and openly urged to learn from their American counterparts. Also, the Soviets show an intense interest in importing a wide range of U. S. technology. In this connection we can be reasonably sure that if given free access to the American market there would be something of a scramble on the part of the Soviets to procure machinery and equipment, including complete plants, embodying the most advanced U. S. technology. Nevertheless, the Soviets seem to be genuinely convinced that in their "system"—with its total power to set priorities, to allocate resources, and to push forward in selected fields without regard to costs or profitability or other economic considerations—they have an immense advantage, that they can in time forge forward to the lasting technological preeminence that they so strongly desire. The 1961 Party Program stated for example:

> "All in all, capitalism is increasingly impeding the development of the contemporary productive forces. Mankind is entering a period of scientific and technical revolution bound up with the conquest of

nuclear energy, space exploration, the development of chemistry, automation and other major achievements of science and engineering. But the relations of production under capitalism are much too narrow for a scientific and technical revolution. Socialism alone is capable of effecting it and applying its fruits in the interest of society. . . .

"Under the socialist system of economy, scientific and technical progress enables man to employ the riches and the forces of nature most effectively in the interest of the people, to discover new forms of energy and to create new materials, to develop means of weather control, and to master outer space. Application of science in production becomes a decisive factor of rapid growth of the productive forces of society. Scientific progress and the introduction of scientific achievements into the economy will remain the object of a special concern to the Party."

Meaning for the U. S.

Economic competition as the Soviets are conducting it on the home front is thus basically a race for technological preeminence. The greatest source of danger to the U. S. in this competition is that the Soviets may succeed in achieving some sort of technological breakthrough, or such a massive overall advance in the technological field as to enable them to effect a broad quantum jump to another power stage—one that might, as the Soviets so fervently hope, put them at long last ahead of the United States, and therewith bring a shift in their favor in the balance of true strategic power. In fact, given the very real limitations under which the Soviets must currently operate in other facets of the struggle they are waging for world supremacy, this may well be the greatest single danger from them that the United States faces.

Chapter Twenty-Six

ECONOMIC COMPETITION
AND THE DEVELOPING AREAS

The second area in which the Soviets rely heavily on economic competition between systems is in their drive for control over the "former colonial countries," their drive to attach to their cause the "intermediate areas of the world." Since 1955 the USSR has placed prime emphasis in its cold war strategy on "winning" the less developed countries through aiding and encouraging them to adopt anti-Western (anti-U. S.) policies and courses, which Moscow calls "truly independent," as a prelude to entry onto a "socialist path." Moscow assertedly sees these countries as the weakest link in the imperialist (U. S.) power chain. It sees them as centers of "stormy national liberation revolutions" which are "sweeping away the colonial system and undermining the foundations of imperialism."

Elements of the Soviet Strategy

The Soviet strategy for capitalizing on the opportunity offered by the spreading "national liberation" movement is lucidly explained, albeit in doctrinal terms, in the 1961 Party Program. The importance of this strategy in the overall Soviet plan of attack justifies noting it in some detail:

> "Young sovereign states have arisen, or are arising, in one-time colonies or semi-colonies. Their peoples have entered a new period of development. They have emerged as makers of a new life and as active participants in world politics, as a revolutionary force destroying imperialism.

> "But the struggle is not yet over. The peoples who are throwing off the shackles of colonialism have attained different degrees of freedom. Many of them, having established national states, are striving for economic and durable political independence. The peoples of those formerly independent countries that in reality depend on foreign monopolies politically and economically are rising to fight against imperialism and reactionary pro-imperialist regimes. The peoples who have not yet cast off their chains of colonial slavery are conducting a heroic struggle against their foreign enslavers. . . .

> "The young sovereign states do not belong either to the system of imperialist states or to the system of socialist states. But the overwhelming majority of them have not yet broken free from the world capitalist economy even though they occupy a special place in it. They constitute that part of the world which is still being exploited by the capitalist monopolies. . . .

> "The existence of the world socialist system and the weakening of imperialism offer the peoples of the newly free countries the prospect of a national renascence, of ending age-long backwardness and poverty, and achieving economic independence. . . .

> "A national liberation revolution does not end with the winning of political independence. Independence will be unstable and will become fictitious unless the revolution brings about radical changes in the social and economic spheres and solves the pressing problems of national rebirth. . . .

> "One of the basic questions confronting these peoples is which road of development the countries that have freed themselves from colonial tyranny are to take, whether the capitalist road or the non-capitalist. . . Socialism is a road to freedom and happiness for the people. It insures rapid economic and cultural progress. It transforms a backward country into an industrial country within the lifetime of one generation and not in the course of centuries. Planned socialist economy is an economy of progress and prosperity by its very nature. Abolition of the exploitation of man by man does away with social inequality. Unemployment disappears completely. Socialism provides all peasants with land, helps them to develop farming, combines their labor efforts

86

in voluntary cooperatives and puts modern agricultural machinery and agronomy at their disposal. Peasant labor is made more productive and the land is made more fertile. Socialism provides a high material and cultural standard of living for the working class and all working people. Socialism lifts the people out of darkness and ignorance and gives them access to modern culture. The intelligentsia is offered ample opportunities for creative efforts for the benefit of the people. . . .

"The establishment and development of *national democracies* open vast prospects for the peoples of the economically undeveloped countries. The political basis of a national democracy is a bloc of all the progressive, patriotic forces fighting to win complete national independence and broad democracy, and to consummate the anti-imperialist, anti-feudal, democratic revolution. . . .

"The socialist countries are sincere and true friends of peoples fighting for their liberation and of those that have freed themselves from the imperialist tyranny, and render them all-around support. . . .

"The Communist Party of the Soviet Union considers fraternal alliance with the peoples who have thrown off colonial or semi-colonial tyranny to be a cornerstone of its international policy. This alliance is based on the common vital interests of world socialism and the world national liberation movement. The Communist Party of the Soviet Union regards it as its international duty to assist the peoples who have set out to win and strengthen their national independence, all peoples who are fighting tor the complete abolition of the colonial system."

"National Democracy": Key New Concept

This strategy involves Soviet reliance upon a new invention of the Soviet theorists: A "national democracy." According to these theorists, a national democracy is at a stage somewhere between a regular capitalist country and a "people's democracy," the term used to designate the second rung of countries in the communist camp (e.g. Hungary, Rumania, Poland, Cuba, etc.).

The theorists have not defined the exact requirements for a country to qualify as a "national democracy." The Party Program suggested such requirements when it stated that the "interests" of a newly emerging country call for:

". . . the eradication of the remnants of colonialism, the elimination of the roots of imperialist power, the ousting of foreign monopolies, the founding of national industry, the abolition of the feudal system and its survival, the implementation of radical land reforms with the participation of the entire peasantry and in its interests, the pursuit of an independent foreign policy of peace, the democratization of the life of society and the strengthening of political independence. . . ."

In practice Moscow seems willing to grant a "national democratic" designation to any country that is outspokenly anti-Western. Also, Moscow stresses that the attainment of a national democratic status is not important in itself; its importance lies in facilitating the advent of "true socialism"; thus the national democratic stage is strictly transitional.

Soviet Operational Techniques and Goals

The role the Soviet Union seeks to play in the developing countries is, first, to secure a combination of forces and a set of policies in particular countries that would make them fit into the "national democracy" mold; and, second, to bring about movement of the national democracies toward a socialist or "people's democracies" status, which requires, of course, membership in the Soviet bloc. To achieve these purposes, the Soviet Union employs a variety of means that fall roughly into a "trade-aid" category.

Building Trade Ties: One of the major means is expanded trade. Between 1955 and 1963, two-way trade between the USSR and the developing countries was increased more than fourfold, from $323 million to $1.435 billion. While this trade has been kept within a "commercial" framework, the Soviets have given it strong artificial encouragement. Most of the machinery and equipment shipped by the Soviet Union, which constitutes the greater part of Soviet exports, has been against long-term credit. Also the Soviet Union has undertaken to give the recipient countries extensive technical and other assistance in utilizing important equipment. In many cases, in fact, imports from the USSR have been part of the implementation of a Soviet masterminded, guided, and underwritten specific developmental project. The Soviet Union has also made special efforts in regard to absorbing the export products of the developing countries. The Soviet leaders have claimed that the USSR because of its social system offers a stable market for any and all of the surpluses of the developing countries, including agricultural and other raw materials, food products, and manufactures. The fact is, however, the regime has encountered great difficulty in making good on this claim, and to a certain extent Soviet imports have amounted to a form of subsidy.

Grant Aid: The Soviets supplement trade and trade credits with direct aid grants to the developing countries. Since the aid grants are ordinarily announced as part of a total package including credits, it is impossible to establish either their exact nature or magnitude. The sum of all Soviet aid grants together with long-term credits appears to total approximately $5 billion over the ten-year period since 1955.

Selective Targeting: Soviet "aid" to the developing countries is carried out on a highly discriminatory basis. Area-wise, concentration is on a few countries that the Soviet Union for one reason or another considers particularly strategic. Thus, more than two-thirds of all Soviet credits and aid grants have gone to four countries: India, Indonesia, Afghanistan, and the United Arab Republic. And more than eighty percent of the remainder to eight others: Iraq, Syria, Algeria, Ethiopia, Ghana, Guinea, Mali, and the Somali Republic. Within each country the Soviet Union places overriding emphasis on projects and undertakings that either produce an impact disproportionate to their cost (such as heavy industry enterprises, stadiums, public buildings and halls, dams, and in some instances airfields and roads), or lend themselves especially well to a direct expansion of Soviet influence (such as mass communication media, schools and technical institutes, research establishments, etc.). A goodly portion of Soviet assistance is in the form of credits to cover the import of Soviet military equipment. Outstanding cases in point are Indonesia, the United Arab Republic, and more recently India. Moscow also moves with alacrity to stimulate and support economic measures and activities which promise to contribute directly to the "economic emancipation" of the developing countries—that is, to undercut western interests and influence and generate frictions with western countries. Examples are measures aimed at the establishment of state control over foreign trade, the expropriation of foreign-owned or -controlled establishments and enterprises, land reforms affecting foreign interests, the nationalization of banking, communication facilities, etc.

Building Soviet Oriented Cadres: One of the interests most stressed by the Soviets in the developing countries is to train a new breed of technicians, public administrators, civil servants, professional personnel, military personnel, etc., who Moscow hopes will take over and run the developing countries in the future. Moscow's aim admittedly is to wean these cadres from western traditions and outlooks and to give them a strictly "socialist" orientation. In recent years, Soviet spokesmen have characterized this training of future leaders as by far the most important aspect of the Soviet design with regard to the developing countries. Moreover, evidence is mounting that activities which serve this cadre training objective in one way or another are being given priority over all others. Some commentaries go so far as to suggest a plan to make this not only the principal but almost the exclusive target of Soviet assistance efforts.

Currently some eight to ten thousand students from Asia, Africa, and Latin America are studying in the universities, professional schools, and technical institutes of the USSR. And this number refers only to students who are receiving a full scale "higher education" in the USSR. In addition, the Soviets have been developing means to give intensive specialized short-term training to tens of thousands of others, primarily in technical fields, within the framework of specific trade-aid agreements, that is, agreements regarding scientific-technical cooperation, the extension of credits, Soviet-managed developmental projects, etc. The particular devices employed under these agreements include: (1) technical schools and training establishments set up in connection with Soviet projects in the developing countries; (2) training programs for technical personnel in Soviet industrial establishments in connection with the supply of plants and equipment to the developing countries; (3) technical high schools and technological institutes founded and staffed by the USSR in the developing countries; and (4) the provision of Soviet technicians to give on-site training to the nationals of developing countries importing complex equipment. Along with formal training efforts along these four lines, the Soviets are placing heavy emphasis on cultural exchanges and contacts. And as a part of its general drive it is of course placing great stress on the training of its own nationals to work effectively with the nationals of the developing countries.

Depth of Soviet Commitment to Trade-Aid Policy

The Soviet program of aiding the developing countries has not been without opposition within the Soviet Union. Considerable restlessness has been revealed at various levels over the expenditure of Soviet resources in those distant lands at a time when the Soviet Union itself has a crying need for more of everything; the failure of the Soviet Union to secure direct returns commensurate with its expenditures has been the subject of criticism at even the highest levels; and note has been taken of the disparity between what the regime is doing for other peoples and what it is doing for the Soviet people themselves. At a meeting of the Soviet Party Central Committee, for example, a high official reported the satisfaction he had felt when he saw Soviet electrical equipment of the finest and most advanced design in a steel mill being built in India. But then he went on to ask: "Is such equipment common in our own factories. Apparently not. Why is this?"

Opposition or no, however, the regime appears thoroughly committed to a continuation of its program for the developing countries. It treats it, in fact, as a cornerstone of Soviet foreign policy. Planning, direction, and administration of the program is centralized in the Council of Ministers of the USSR itself. A special committee within the Council, the State Committee for Economic Relations with Foreign Countries, is in direct and full charge.

Meaning for the U. S.

The *scale* of Soviet operations in the developing countries, despite the breadth and many sidedness, is not such as to justify great concern on the part of the United States. The Soviet program pales in comparison with the U. S. program which it seeks to parallel. Further, its heavy concentration on a small number of countries greatly reduces the range of its challenge. Insofar as the operations are conducted on the basis of economic competition in the normal sense of that expression, the United States is thoroughly capable of coping with them. In fact, in a straight competition the U. S. has almost every conceivable advantage. We have far greater resources. We have experience. We do not seek anything for ourselves. We do not try to "take over."

The Soviets, however, and this goes almost without saying, do their best to avoid playing the game on a strict "economic competition" basis. The Soviets seek a direct interjection through economic means of communists and communist sympathizers into positions of decisive influence in the target countries. Their efforts, despite the doctrinal trappings with which they cover them, represent an extension and refinement of time-honored communist techniques for penetration, subversion, and control.

Moscow's object, as Soviet spokesmen clearly and frankly explain, is not the solution of problems within the developing countries, but the creation of conditions and movements within those countries that will take them along the path toward a communist system and membership in the Soviet Bloc. The aim is, as the Soviets themselves say, conquest— conquest to be sure through other than traditional means but conquest nevertheless. Certain of the things the Soviets have done in the developing countries, if they could be taken in isolation, would be welcome to the United States and other forward-looking countries. But even the constructive accomplishments are subjoined in a purpose that has as its end subverting the established order and with that undermining Western interests, particularly the interests of the United States.

A German analyst, Dr. Curt Gasteyger, has highlighted the meaning for the Western world of the Soviet drive in the developing countries. Writing in the August, 1962 issue of *Survey,* Dr. Gasteyger said:

> "All this [activity of the Soviets] may be in sharp contrast to the revolutionary fervor of the 1920s; on the other hand, there is no doubt that, especially among the developing countries, the communist economic and social program serves as a substitute, or support for a unified political dogma. The continuing social revolutionary process in this area is the real motor of the communist movement. . . . Soviet engagement in the developing regions of the world has merely multiplied the areas of conflict with the West. While Stalin was fairly

91

reluctant and unable to produce a series of simultaneous crises, Khrushchev's strategy, to use Philip Mosley's term, appears to be that of the rolling crisis. It is by no means certain that Moscow will always be able to keep the strategy under its control, and if one looks upon its policy vis-a-vis the developing countries with this aspect in mind, it is not easy to feel particularly optimistic about the future course; or quite certain about the outcome of the present one."

Chapter Twenty-Seven

FROM "ECONOMIC COMPETITION" IN THE DEVELOPING COUNTRIES TO "WARS OF LIBERATION"

The events that have transpired over the three years since Dr. Gasteyger voiced these thoughts have given substance to the danger he sensed.

First, there was the attempt on the part of the Soviet leaders to use the position they had secured in one of the developing countries, Cuba, to turn directly and militarily against the United States.

Second, and posing a more enduring danger, the Soviet campaign to win to the communist cause "the intermediate areas of the world" has become increasingly intertwined with a new and highly dangerous form of military aggression, the so-called "wars of liberation."

Why Focus on Wars of Liberation?

The matter of "wars of liberation" may seem foreign to the subject matter of this study. However, these wars are now, and may well be for the indefinite future, the crux of the struggle between the communist and noncommunist worlds, particularly the struggle between the communists and the United States. Therefore, they are a matter which can hardly be left out in any consideration of a change in one of the basic U. S. policies directed toward the USSR. The weight that should be given to the growing immersion of the Soviet program of "economic competition in the developing countries" in the war of liberation movement is not something that needs to be decided at this point. But we at least need to be aware of what is taking place and to consider its implications for our own strategy.

Former Secretary of State Dean Acheson has said that wars of liberation are conflicts in which "armed forces are engaged, men are being killed and wounded, villages are destroyed, noncombatants killed and impoverished. All that mankind has known as war for centuries is being waged." From this point we need to go on and recognize that these wars are being waged against the United States itself. And this is speaking literally, not figuratively. South Vietnam, for example, is a pawn of a pawn in a larger contest the communists are waging directly and immediately against the United States.

Enmeshment of the USSR in a Chinese Communist Design

The communist aim is to destroy the strong through the weak. The Soviet Union has one schema. Communist China another. But despite the differences, the antagonisms, and rivalry between Communist China and the Soviet Union, the plan and activities of the one react upon the plan and activities of the other. It may well be that the Soviet Union would prefer, as Soviet theoretical commentaries assert, to avoid outside participation in the "liberation struggle" within a particular country. However, the Soviet Union has ceased to be a free agent in the matter The Communist Chinese keep the Soviets under constant and vicious attack over the war of liberation issue. They use any evidence of Soviet caution as grounds for charges that the Soviet Party has turned its back on "Marxism-Leninism" and joins with the "imperialists" in efforts to keep "enslaved peoples" enslaved. While Moscow subjects the Chinese to equally devastating countercharges, with matching vehemence and vitriol, at the same time it finds it necessary to go further and further to demonstrate its continued ardent support for the world revolutionary cause. Thus a Khrushchev-initiated line that, "with the present balance of world forces," armed conflict is not a prerequisite for the triumph of communism on a world scale, has had to be steadily modified to make an exception for "wars of liberation." Where the Soviets once talked of the necessity of avoiding "little wars," wherever they might occur and regardless of circumstances, because of the danger they would grow into a "big war" that would destroy all mankind, they now not only condone but speak strongly in favor of "little wars" that aim at "national liberation."

The Soviet program for achieving a "peaceful" conquest of the intermediate areas of the world through winning an "economic competition between systems" has in consequence taken on an entirely new coloration. While Moscow continues to insist its approach is radically different from the Chinese, it in fact increasingly reflects Chinese postulates and is more and more shaped by Chinese decisions. A one-time supposition that for the future the USSR might follow "a high road" toward communist goals while Communist China followed a "low road" appears to have less and less validity. To keep the Chinese from taking over the world movement, the Soviets have had to adjust to standards set by the Chinese. Peking calls the tune and Moscow willy-nilly has to dance to it, albeit with reluctance and under protest.

The Strategic Use of Wars of Liberation

To understand, therefore, what we really face in the "economic competition between systems" in the developing countries we need to understand what the Chinese communists are up to and how this intermeshes with and shapes Soviet plans and activities.

Peking sees the problem of defeating the United States as essentially the same problem they faced earlier with Chiang's Nationalist Government in China itself. And they have the same solution: to make continuing guerrilla war on the United States through a succession of guerrilla attacks (in the guise of the "wars of liberation") on particular points in the U. S. power structure, beginning with the most vulnerable and moving up the scale as repeated defeats sap the strength and will of the U. S. and build that of the communists. Basic to this strategy are:

(1) *The "paper tiger" concept*: U. S. power, even as Nationalist power, has "feet of clay" in that it does not have the support of the "subjected peoples" at home and abroad on which its existence depends, and in that those who wield it do not have either the faith or the will necessary to defend their cause against resolute attack.

(2) *Asia, Africa, and Latin America constitute the Achilles' heel of U. S. power*: "These are the most vulnerable areas under imperialist [i.e. United States] rule. . . . Revolutionary struggles of the people in Asia, Africa, and Latin America are pounding and undermining the foundations of [American] rule. . . . In a sense, therefore, the whole cause of the international proletarian revolution hinges on the outcome of the revolutionary struggles of the people of these areas. . . ."

(3) *The essence of these struggles is war*: "Wars of liberation" . . . these large-scale and small-scale revolutionary wars against the imperialists [Americans] and their lackeys. . . . Political power grows out of the barrel of a gun. . . . The seizure of power by armed force, the settlement of the issue by war, is the central task and highest form of revolution . . . . It is only by the power of the gun that the working class and laboring masses can defeat the armed bourgeoise and the landlords . . . only with guns can the whole world be transformed. . . ."

(4) *Wars of liberation, that is, revolutionary attacks on U. S. position, do not occur of themselves, they must be promoted*: " . . . full use must be made of the very favorable situation [that now exists] . . . and in light of the specific conditions in different countries the development of revolutionary struggle [wars of liberation] must be actively promoted and preparations made to seize victory in the revolution. . . . The socialist countries must become base areas for supporting and develop-

ing the revolution of the oppressed nations and peoples throughout the world; [they must] form the closest alliance with them and carry the proletarian world revolution through to completion."

(5) *The United States will not react with the fullness of its power against the use of wars of liberation because of fear of general war, which "it knows will bring the final destruction of capitalism."* The United States will instead play the game according to the rules laid down by the communists, either beating a humiliating retreat or fighting a losing fight at places of communist choosing, with weapons of communist choosing, at the tempo of communist choosing: "However hard the imperialists [Americans] bestir themselves . . . the victory of the national liberation revolution is irresistible. . . . The logic of the imperialists [Americans] is to make trouble, fail, make trouble again, fail again . . . till their doom."

Where Chinese Strategy and Soviet Strategy Mesh

The Soviet leaders strongly reject the rationale that underlies the individual points on which the Chinese communists base their war of liberation strategy. Yet when it comes to the key assumption of the Chinese strategy—that the United States will not risk global war to save a non-vital position—Soviet views move very close to the Chinese.

Basically, the Russians and the Chinese both bet on an inability of the U. S to bridge the gap between a localized reaction in kind, where U. S. costs are greatest and U. S. effectiveness least, and a nuclear strike reaction, where the consequences for the U. S. itself would be so far-reaching as to make it unthinkable in any but the most extreme case. Each, in other words, assumes aggressions can be undertaken without any greater cost to itself than would be required to keep the aggression going in the local area chosen, without any greater risk than that the aggression in question might fail. The Russians allow that an aggression must stop short of a regular war involving state forces, but this is seen not as an invalidation of the assumption, but as a requirement for care and circumspection in the execution of an aggression. As long as direct provocation is avoided, the U. S. will accept changes, no matter how farreaching or harmful to U. S. interests. The U. S., the Soviets insist, will not dare to risk "exporting counterrevolution." (Moscow, for example, has consistently explained the U. S. failure to crush Castro in just these terms.)

The Chinese allow that at some point an aggression might lead the U. S. to take the plunge into general war, but this would not be because the assumption was wrong but because the overall struggle with the U. S. had reached the stage where the U. S. would be desperately flailing out in a final but vain effort to save its system from destruction.

An Enduring Factor in U.S.-Soviet Relations

The "War of Liberation" that currently is so endangering U. S. security—the war in South Vietnam—is of Chinese Communist doing. The Soviet leaders very probably wish that the affair had never gotten started, or that it will somehow simply go away. They stand to lose whichever wins, Communist China or the United States. However, the "laws of history" in which they have such faith give them no choice but to be a supporter of the communist side in the struggle. And the "laws of history" will almost certainly force a repetition of the pattern as other wars of liberation are precipitated. Given this orientation, a very basic question arises for the United States: how meaningful is the distinction that is so often and so carefully drawn between the Soviet Union and the more virulent of the communist states? To ask this question is not to suggest the answer. It is only to suggest an added and obviously important reason for keeping the review of our policies against the USSR within the context of the broad strategies that are operating on each side and the total requirements that are upon us at this stage of the struggle in which we are so deeply engaged.

PART 6

THE SPECIAL PROBLEM OF THE NON-SOVIET COMMUNIST COUNTRIES

The United States has three distinct trade policies toward the non-Soviet communist countries.

One applies to those countries of Eastern Europe that remain full-fledged Soviet satellites. These include, at the time of this writing, East Germany, Czechoslovakia, Hungary and Bulgaria. The United States treats these as it treats the USSR, on the assumption that any benefit to them is automatically a benefit for the USSR.

A second applies to those of the East European communist countries that have shown a greater or lesser degree of national assertiveness as against the USSR in either external affairs or internal affairs or both. These include—so far—Yugoslavia, Poland, and Rumania. "National assertiveness" among these three differs widely and U. S. policy toward them varies accordingly. Thus this second policy breaks down in practice into three subpolicies, of which the Yugoslavian is the most "liberal," the Polish next, and the Rumanian least.

The third aims at those communist countries which, whatever their relationship with the USSR, represent a special threat or problem for the United States. These include Communist China, North Vietnam, North Korea, and Cuba. Against these the United States enforces a near total embargo based upon the Trading with the Enemy Act. Albania, which has broken almost completely with the USSR and voluntarily assumed a puppet role with regard to Communist China, is not a member of the embargoed group. Technically, it is free to trade with the U. S. on the same terms as the USSR and its satellites. However, the U. S. does not maintain diplomatic relations with Albania, and by default, as it were, trade between the two countries is mutually embargoed.

Why these differing policies? "If," as Secretary of State Rusk asked in an address quoted extensively below, "the communists, as a group, have as their aim the destruction of our way of life, how is it that we can treat one communist country differently from another? And why do we enter into an understanding with a communist government over one matter, while accepting the hard necessity of continued hostility and conflict over other matters?"

The answer to this question lies in (a) our unwillingness to accept as final the extension of the Soviet system into non-Soviet areas, (b) our conviction that within the nations subjected to communist rule increasingly strong forces work against the perpetuation of that rule, and (c) our belief that we can through our own policies and conduct both encourage those forces and increase the chances for their success.

In some cases we seek to exercise influence by working against a regime; in others by working through a regime. In principle, our choice is dependent on the behavior of the regime in question. In practice, a variety of other considerations enter. With respect to Cuba, for example, our stated policy is to reject accommodation to a communist regime simply because it is a communist regime, and presumably regardless of how it may conduct itself. The same is essentially true with regard to Communist China, at least up to the time of this writing. In the final analysis, the factor that determines our willingness or unwillingness to adjust our policies to changing behavior on the part of a particular communist regime is whether that regime *in itself* constitutes a menace to U. S. interests or whether it serves only as a medium through which the Soviet Union menaces them.

Chapter Twenty-Eight

THE CASE OF THE NON-SOVIET COMMUNIST STATES OF EASTERN EUROPE

The United States, in practical terms, has always viewed the danger posed by the lesser communist regimes of Eastern Europe as a simple extension of the danger posed by the Soviet Union. While deploring the harsh fate of the peoples subject to the rule of those regimes, U. S. policies have aimed not so much against the regimes themselves as against their serving the power interests of the USSR. Consequently, the U. S. has consistently, and over four administrations, shown a ready willingness to adjust its policies if and as any one of the regimes gives convincing signs of self-assertiveness as against the Soviet Union and its dictates regarding either internal or external matters.

Why and How We Treat the Different Communist Countries of Eastern Europe Differently

Secretary of State Dean Rusk in a February, 1964, address before a

Conference of the International Union of Electrical Workers, succinctly explained the nature of our policies and the underlying rationale. His remarks merit recalling in some detail:

"We believe that the peoples who have been brought under Communist rule aspire to a better life—of peace, economic opportunity, and a chance to pursue happiness. This, indeed, has always been so. But in recent years an important new trend has been perceptible: Some of the Communist governments have become responsive, in varying degrees, if not directly to the aspirations of their subjects, at least to kindred aspirations of their own. The Communist world is no longer a single flock of sheep following blindly behind one leader."

* * *

"The smaller Communist countries of Eastern Europe have increasingly, although in varying degree, asserted their own policies. We have always considered it unnatural for the diverse peoples of Eastern Europe, with their own talents and proud traditions, to be submerged in a monolithic bloc. We have wanted these peoples, while living in friendship with their Russian and other neighbors, to develop in accordance with their own national aspirations and genius. And they seem to feel a strong nostalgia for their traditional ties with the West. Most of them are increasing their trade and other contacts with Western Europe and, to some extent, with us."

* * *

"When Yugoslavia challenged Stalin's centralized control of Communist affairs in 1948, we gave that country military and economic assistance. Yugoslavia not only defied Stalin but stopped supporting the guerrilla aggression against Greece, reached an agreement with Italy on Trieste, and increased its economic, political, and cultural ties with the West. It is not a member of the Warsaw Pact. As a non-aligned state, it has gained influence among the uncommitted nations of the world. Sometimes it agrees with the Soviet Union on particular points of foreign policy, sometimes not. In brief, Yugoslavia is an independent state. Its success in defending its independence made other peoples in Eastern Europe wonder why they could not do likewise. And not least important from our viewpoint, Yugoslavia is not shipping arms to be used against a democratic government in Venezuela and is not trying to destroy non-Communist governments in South Viet-Nam and Laos."

* * *

"For some years we have treated Poland somewhat differently from other Soviet bloc states. A good deal of the national autonomy and domestic liberalization which the Poles won in 1956 persists. Most of Polish agriculture remains in private hands; religion is strong; Poland has developed a broad range of relations and exchanges with the West. Poland has historic ties with the West. And its people are the close blood relatives of many citizens of the United States. We apologize to none for our efforts to help the brave people of Poland to preserve their national identity and their own aspirations."

* * *

"Thus, for good reasons, we have treated various Soviet bloc states

99

differently. . . . And we shall continue to differentiate our policy according to the conduct of the various Communist states."

* * *

"Recently Rumania has asserted a more independent attitude and has expanded its trade and other contacts with the West. It has taken steps to improve its relations with the United States. We are responding accordingly."

* * *

"Hungary has turned to a more permissive policy of national conciliation. We, of course, welcome any tendencies promising to ease the lot of the Hungarian people. We will do what we can to encourage them."

* * *

"In Czechoslovakia and Bulgaria there are some signs of movement away from earlier and harsher policies. We are watching these developments with close attention."

Pro and Con Attitudes and Arguments

Strong voices have often been raised against these "differential" policies. On one occasion—and following on a grossly distorted apology for Soviet policies by Tito at a "Non-Aligned Conference" held in Belgrade in September 1961—the Congress importantly curtailed the discretionary authority on the basis of which the Administration granted concessions to Yugoslavia and Poland. The authority—which related to most-favored-nation treatment for the two nations—was later restored, but only after a bitter and prolonged legislative struggle.

The division of opinion regarding the policies arises from differing views as to the principal source of the danger posed by communism. Those in opposition focus on the communist movement as an ideological movement; those favoring the policies see as the main threat the USSR and the power base it commands. The one argues that any communist state, whether responsive to Soviet control or not, adds strength to the communist cause which is necessarily and irrevocably hostile to the United States and all it stands for; the other that a communist state that asserts its independence of Moscow not only reduces the direct power commanded by the USSR, but weakens the communist cause itself in that it contributes to a shattering of the monolithic character on which the effectiveness of the movement depends.

If it is conceded that it is indeed in the interest of the U. S. for the Soviet East-European empire to be broken up even at cost of favorable U. S. treatment for dissident communist states, then an important policy question arises that is highly germane to the main issue examined in this study, namely, the issue of whether the U. S. should or should not liberalize its trade policies toward the USSR. Is there not a basic inconsistency between the rationale for differential policies based upon the demonstration by puppet states of "national assertiveness" as against the USSR and the rationale for relaxed policies toward the USSR itself? If our object is to erode the structure of Soviet power in Eastern Europe, how can this be reconciled with a blanket extension of better trade relations to all of the countries of Eastern Europe, irrespective of the degree of subservience to the USSR, and even to the USSR itself?

The Problem of Economic Integration of the Soviet European Bloc

An aspect of this matter that merits special attention relates to the problem of the economic integration of the Soviet European Bloc. As rapidly as Soviet sway was extended over the countries of Eastern Europe after the war, the orientation of trade and economic life generally was shifted from West to East. The responsible factor was, of course, the dictate of the Soviet government. Stalin saw his acquisitions as conquests, and he made little effort to disguise the ruthlessness with which he exploited them. Using various devices, which ranged from "reparation" payments on the part of "former enemy countries" to Soviet dominated "joint stock companies," he denuded the satellites of much of their capital goods and forced production into patterns that would best serve the needs of the USSR. Stalin in his turn supplied the satellites with products necessary to keep production for the USSR going, but on terms highly favorable to the USSR.

Gradually, Soviet exploitation became less direct and more subtle. Under Soviet direction, each of the satellites began its own program of "socialist construction" on the Soviet model. But with few exceptions developmental projects were tailored more to Soviet than satellite requirements. And swarms of Soviet advisers and experts were distributed at key points at every level in each of the satellites to insure that performance went according to Soviet plans.

The satellites under these conditions were an enormous asset to the USSR. No means exist for measuring with any exactness their contribution to Soviet postwar "reconstruction" and to the rapid growth of Soviet industry that followed reconstruction. But clearly the contribution was great indeed. However, the asset represented by the satellites proved perishable, eventually in fact counterproductive. The years after the death of Stalin became a time of reckoning. Economic deterioration of the satellites became so acute as to face the USSR with a choice between accepting a virtual reversal of economic roles and allowing the satellites to become lasting political liabilities.

Moscow has reluctantly, haltingly, and sparingly gone along with assistance to the satellites. However, while doing so it has still sought to shape the developmental process so as to perpetuate the dependence of the satellites on the USSR, and, more important, to establish on a new and firmer basis "cooperative" arrangements that would have the effect of once again enabling the Soviets to draw great and increasing strength from the satellite economies.

Using the machinery devised by Stalin in 1949 to serve as a communist counterweight to the Marshall Plan—the "Council for Economic Mutual Assistance"—the Soviet leaders have over the past several years, and especially since 1962, attempted to achieve the economic integration of the European Bloc on a scale and in a way that would bring about an effective "division of labor," with the Soviet Union serving as the pivotal point in division arrangements. The satellites, however, have successfully resisted these efforts. Each has shown a willingness to "cooperate," but only to the extent that it would benefit at the expense of its partners, including the USSR.

A factor that has enabled the individual satellites to resist Soviet pressures has been the growing opportunity for bilateral trade with western countries. This raises a question which requires serious pondering. What would be the effect of a U. S. decision to move to a new trade relationship with the European Bloc on a blanket basis? It would seem obvious that further steps by the U. S. to improve trade with particular countries that demonstrate "national assertiveness" as against the USSR would strengthen resistance to the integration process. But what if the United States abandoned the practice of distinguishing among the satellites, or between the satellites and the USSR?

Chapter Twenty-Nine
THE CASE OF COMMUNIST CHINA

Why a Trade Embargo?

"We have special and very grave concerns about Communist China . . . . When Mainland China has a government which is prepared to renounce force, to make peace, and to honor international responsibilities, it will find us responsive. . . . Meanwhile we shall resolutely oppose aggression. And we believe all free nations should, in their own elementary self-interest, take care not to do anything that would encourage Communist [China's] militancy."

In these words Secretary Rusk stated the philosophy that underlies the U. S. embargo of trade with Communist China and U. S. efforts to get other free nations to join in that embargo. The U. S. instituted the embargo in 1950 in consequence of the Korean War. The U. S. has continued it since on grounds that the Peking regime persists in the policies that led to its condemnation by the United Nations as an aggressor. More particularly, the regime refuses to forego the use of force in respect of the Formosan problem; menaces India and Thailand; insists upon the right of North Korea to "reunify" Korea by force if necessary; and actively supports the North Vietnamese in their attacks on South Vietnam.

The U. S. has, however, a larger purpose than the end of the immediate military threats posed by China. As indicated by Rusk in the above quotation, our trade embargo is a part of a general policy of attempted isolation of mainland China unless and until the communist government collapses or goes through a basic change in attitudes, purposes and conduct. Other elements of this general policy include nonrecognition, opposition to U. N. membership, and a ban on travel. And the whole is backed up by continued U. S. treatment of the Nationalist Government on Taiwan as the legitimate government of China.

Currently, little pressure is being exerted on the trade embargo or other parts of the U. S. China policy. Some years back, glowing accounts of communist successes in building a new economic and social order, coupled with mounting Chinese prestige and influence abroad, produced a widespread sense of failure for U. S. efforts, but no strong movement developed for a change in course. A few scattered voices urged an "adjustment to reality," but the consensus seemed more inclined toward passive resignation to a China prospering in isolation from the U. S. than toward a search for alternatives.

The one instance in which serious consideration was given to breaking the trade embargo came as an aftermath of the series of disastrous Chinese harvests beginning in 1959-60. The Chinese authorities became so sorely pressed as to take the unprecedented step of making large purchases of wheat from Canada, Australia, Argentina, and other western suppliers. In time rumors circulated of feelers by a Peking intermediary in Hong Kong regarding the U. S. market. The rumors never became firm enough to force a U. S. decision. (In point of fact they were without foundation, evidently representing a "trial balloon" operation by an enterprising U. S. export firm.) Thought nevertheless was given to a possible favorable response in the hope of getting Peking off dead center in its hostility toward the U. S. and onto a negotiations track. Some went even further and suggested the U. S. use its surplus grain in a mammoth trade off of "food for peace." Partly to quiet domestic speculation and partly to make clear that direct initiatives by the Chinese government would be necessary for any U. S. decision, President

Kennedy told a press conference in the summer of 1962 that no Chinese request for an export license for grain was before the government and no decision could be taken one way or another unless one were submitted. In the end, Peking rather than Washington laid the whole matter to rest, publicly and scornfully ruling out any interest in the purchase of grain or anything else from the U. S.

The turn of events since this episode—and particularly the Chinese military attack on India, the growing flagrance of the Chinese supported North Vietnamese aggression against South Vietnam, and the Chinese explosion of an atomic device, plus evidence of internal difficulties in China—has served to quiet misgivings regarding the correctness of U. S. policy. Seldom in the current debate over East-West trade has a voice been raised in favor of easing the embargo against China.

Policies of Other Western Countries

Meanwhile, a steady improvement has been taking place in trade relations between Communist China and the other major western powers. This has been due in part to a relaxation by western governments; it has been due more to a change in Chinese policies.

The most important slippage that has occurred in the western camp relates to Japan. The Japanese have always professed to see the main communist danger as lying in the USSR. As long as China appeared firmly locked in with the Soviets, Tokyo's sense of alarm was maximal. But a Peking in conflict with Moscow is seen as an entirely different matter.

The Japanese view the Chinese communists as somehow a different sort of communist. They question whether, either over the short or long term, China by itself poses a genuine threat to such of its neighbors as have their own house in order. In any event, they do not doubt their own ability to understand and to deal with the "China problem." And they see in the break between China and the USSR a great opportunity: First, to influence China to follow an essentially different and less dangerous road than the Soviets; second, to build over time a close economic interdependence between themselves and the Chinese, an interdependence reminiscent of the economic attributes envisaged for the "Greater East Asia Co-prosperity Sphere." Japan still withholds recognition from Peking and in other ways maintains a facade of political aloofness. But behind the facade, the nation has positioned itself to establish an entirely new trade relationship.

The great significance of the Japanese shift lies, of course, in the capacity of Japan to supply sophisticated equipment and even to underwrite the development of important Chinese industries. Tokyo's stance raises as serious possibilities long-term credits and far-reaching barter arrangements. The Chinese, for their part, have not moved to capitalize on the full readiness of Japan to trade. They have, however, stepped up their purchases in Japan and they have made gestures suggestive of an intention to move at some point to far bigger things. Significantly, these gestures include the virtual dropping of the "political conditions" previously insisted upon as a prerequisite for increased trade.

France's recognition of Communist China admittedly carried with it a willingness, in fact a strong hope, for improved and expanded trade relations. The Chinese have "explored" purchase possibilities in France with some fanfare, but the main results to date have been the whetting of French appetites.

The British, West Germans and Italians also seek increased trade with the Chinese, although there is a certain wariness with regard to credits. Canada, Argentina and Australia have welcomed Chinese purchases of grain, purchases which in the case of Canada at least have made significant economic impact. Sales in each case involve credits, but so far on a commercial basis.

Easing of U. S. Pressures on Friendly Governments

As the other western states have moved to bring their trade policies toward China into harmony with those followed for the USSR and the East-European communist states, the U. S. has evidently relaxed the special efforts it long exerted to hold the line as firmly as possible against the Chinese. To an extent this represents a bowing to the inevitable: The U. K. has consistently refused to limit sales in accord with U. S. wishes; Canada flatly rejected U. S. cautions re wheat sales; the Japanese have insisted they know the Chinese and how to deal with them better than the U. S.; and France completely ignored the U. S. in connection with the establishment of diplomatic relations and the accompanying trade overtures. At the same time, however, the curtailment of U. S. pressures has apparently been interpreted by some friendly governments as tacit U. S. agreement to increased trade and as a possible harbinger of a change in the policy of the U. S. itself.

Reorientation of China's Trade Toward the West

From the Chinese side, a truly spectacular shift in trade patterns has occurred. This, of course, has been primarily due to the break with the

USSR. But an important contributing factor has been an altered internal situation and outlook.

The Shift to Socialist Trade: Once in power in 1949, the communists sought as a matter of deliberate design to divert trade from China's traditional partners to the USSR and the lesser communist states. One factor was simple political preference, a preference expressed by Mao's "lean to one side policy." Another was a conviction, based not on experience but ideological faith, that a Soviet product, as the product of a "socialist order," was necessarily superior to any other. Finally, the Chinese expected the Russians to meet them more than half way, and as comrades in a common cause to give generously of their resources to help China move rapidly from "feudalism" to modernity.

Trade between China and the other communist countries, and primarily with the USSR, increased from under 5 percent of the Chinese total prior to the communist take-over to 25 percent in 1950 and to over seventy-five percent in 1955. There was a leveling off of the communist share between 1956 and 1960, but it remained above the seventy percent mark. Meanwhile, the composition of trade changed greatly. China's exports remained standard, but imports were increasingly taken up with the machinery and equipment and complete plants required for the regime's ambitious modernization program. (This was the period when Mao and his associates attempted to follow as closely as possible the "Soviet model" for both industrialization and collectivization. It was also the period of close and direct Soviet technical guidance.)

Turning to the West: Beginning in 1960 and continuing unbrokenly since, a sharp reversal has taken place. Trade with other communist countries fell from some 70 percent of China's total in 1959 to less than 45 percent in 1963. A further drop occurred in 1964 and advance indications suggest a total of around 30 percent in 1965. Thus within a decade and a half the pendulum of China's trade has swung from almost complete free world domination over to communist domination and back to free world domination. Regarding the Soviet Union alone, trade moved from a negligible quantity prior to 1949 to over $2 billion in 1959 and back to less than $500 million in 1964. For 1965 China's total trade with the USSR will probably be well under the $350 million it will exchange with Britain's crown colony of Hong Kong.

Why the Change: Both politics and economics contributed to the breakdown of Sino-Soviet trade relationships, and while each blamed the other, both were responsible. Moreover, both had good reason to welcome the development. Moscow took the first overt steps when, in 1959, it reneged on a weapons technology agreement, and, in 1960, withdrew the Soviet technicians—with blueprints, etc.—who were aiding the Chinese development efforts. Moscow's action was precipitated by carping Chinese attacks on Soviet policies, but the decision came at a time when Chinese economic requirements and demands were bearing increasingly heavily on the USSR. The Chinese complained bitterly over Soviet "highhandedness" and "lack of good faith," but they at the same time gave evidence of disenchantment over both the efficacy of Soviet aid efforts and the quality of Soviet goods. Further, Peking was in the midst of an economic crisis that precluded continued concentration on the industrialization efforts for which Soviet goods were being procured and with which Soviet technicians were principally helping.

Change in Purposes of Trade

Coincident with the economic break with the Soviets, Peking made a sweeping change in the composition of its imports. Machinery and equipment items dropped precipitously; the regime not only stopped placing orders in the USSR and the European satellites, it cancelled out many orders against which production was already well underway. It at the same time reduced purchases of industrial products from Western Europe by 75 percent. Buying was concentrated on grain, fertilizers, petroleum products, and the raw materials needed for China's traditional export industries.

Initially it was assumed that the new pattern of imports would continue only until acute crisis conditions were overcome, and that there would then be a revived drive for the items needed for industrial development. Yet the pattern has persisted and the regime still gives no indication of an early change. Extensive inquiries are made regarding procurement possibilities for heavy equipment in various western markets, but actual orders are few and far between. And most of these are related to the light industries that furnish traditional exports or to industries supporting agriculture.

Incongruity of Current Chinese Practices

This all adds up to a seemingly strange situation for China as a communist country. The regime disdains economic ties with the USSR and the other European communist countries, and in doing so shatters the communist "world market" in which Stalin and others vested such great hopes, and it closes to itself any prospect of getting the developmental assistance it so badly needs. The regime also has placed on ice, if it has not in effect abandoned, the cardinal internal objective dictated by the Marxist-Leninist-Stalinist creed, to which the regime professes such devotion, that is, the rapid development of a heavy industry base on which to build a "socialist system." It uses foreign exchange to procure food for immediate consumption and to get raw materials and machinery to produce goods for export in order to buy more food and more raw materials, et cetera, a practice which is about as alien to a Leninist-Stalinist model as it could be.

The simple truth of the matter is that Peking has taken in the conduct of its internal affairs and in its separatist trade policies a thoroughgoing "revisionist" course.

The Meaning for the U. S.

What does this suggest for the United States? Is there a handle here which, as the Japanese and others argue, can be manipulated to work Peking further and further away from communist norms and closer and closer to western? If the Chinese conduct trade to free themselves from dependence on the USSR and other "socialist countries," and if it concentrates trade on sectors that have to do with consumption and building capabilities to compete with its exports under marketplace conditions, should not the United States itself have a try at the trade game?

Given the present situation, these questions have an academic ring. With American forces engaged in bloody combat in South Vietnam against communists manipulated and directed from Peking, any U. S. trade with China is obviously unthinkable. But what if there should be a change in immediate circumstances? Would the questions not then take on great force? Should, for example, Peking be brought to a willingness to negotiate a settlement of the Vietnamese conflict, would a new trade policy not come to seem a good bargaining counter for the U. S. to put on the table?

As we give consideration to this matter, it is most important that we understand what is really going on in China and what it is all about. The following points particularly merit attention:

1. *The Peking regime has not halted its drive to build a Stalinist-type economic order by choice, but by necessity.* It imports food rather than machinery because it has to. It leaves heavy industry establishments half completed and permits cobwebs to gather on once treasured plans because it is forced to use all the resources it can command simply to keep the country's head above water. It is mired down in difficulties that defy solution. The crisis conditions that followed on the disastrous failures of the "great leap" have been moderated, but only through the

108

sacrifice of developmental goals. Meanwhile the fundamental problems that produced the crisis remain unresolved.

These fundamental problems, it is important to emphasize, were not generated, as is sometimes said, by the mistakes and excesses of the "great leap." As a matter of fact, the origins of the "great leap" effort lay in the presence and persistence of the problems, rather than the reverse. The story, which is vital to an understanding of the outlook regarding China, can be simply told:

China made striking progress during the first three or so years after the communists seized power in 1949. The responsible factors were the restoration of order after some twenty years of civil and interstate war; the establishment of a more effective central administration; some badly needed house-cleaning reforms; and renewed vigor on the part of the population due to improved working conditions combined with rising expectations of better things to come. And for the first time China was able to benefit from the heavy industry base built by Japan in Manchuria. Little, if anything, was at play in the way of peculiar communist techniques and programs. The upsurge came from the establishment of conditions that enabled the industrious Chinese people to exercise in traditional ways their great skill and talents. A built-in ceiling existed, however, on just how much could be accomplished in this manner. The system could only be made to work better; it could not be transformed. And the new rulers wanted to transform it. They wanted to duplicate in China the "socialist construction" achievements of the USSR.

Beginning in 1952-53, therefore, the regime began to apply in China the Stalinist model for development, including forced draft collectivization, centralized planning, ruthless concentration on a heavy industry base, etc. Results, however, were disappointing. The Soviet book (more particularly Stalin's *Short Course* on the history of the Soviet Party) was followed almost to the letter, and Soviet experience directly tapped in the form of a horde of technicians and political advisers as well as heavy imports of Soviet machinery, equipment and complete plants. China, however, proved to be something quite different from the Soviet Union. It lacked the base that had been built up in Russia during more than a generation of rapid industrialization prior to the Bolshevik triumph; even more important, it had a highly adverse land-population ratio while the Soviets had had a highly favorable one.

By 1957 Peking became aware that the Soviet way was not going to work for China. A painful search consequently began for a different way—a Chinese way—that could serve better to thrust China forward into the twentieth century. The solution decided upon was the trilogy of

"the general line," "the great leap," and "the communes." The scheme
was quite direct. The greatest of China's resources, its vast hordes of
people, would be marshaled and driven to pull China up by its boot-
straps. What could not be done by centralized planning and attempted
mechanization would be accomplished by harnessing and exploiting the
energies of China's hundreds of millions of men, women, and children.
Through utilizing human labor on an unprecedented scale and at an unprecedented intensity agricultural yields would be multiplied, vast dams
and roads built, cities and villages transformed, industrial production
pushed to fantastic levels.

The Chinese way of the great leap worked even less well than the
Russian way of Stalin. It brought the country to the verge of ruin. For
some five years now the regime has had to devote its resources and energies to digging the country out of the wreckage and debris produced
by the "mad experiment."

The problem has been not simply a matter of getting the country back
"on course." The course that was being followed *before* the experiment
was itself not bringing about the progress required for the modernization of China. In spite of the humiliating retreats of the leadership and
the relatively desperate palliatives to which it has resorted, China remains a great sprawling underdeveloped country wallowing in the mire
of age-old problems and difficulties, of which the most acute relate to
the "too many people, too little land, too few resources" situation. The
only way in which substantial change could be brought about would be
through truly massive assistance from the outside, assistance on a scale
that would severely tax a USSR or even a U. S. Lacking such outside
assistance, the country must plod along as best it can, making slow progress at one time and slipping back at another, even perhaps to the
brink of disaster, depending on the vagaries of nature, on the one hand,
and the ability of the rulers to exercise restraints on their ambitions, on
the other. The regime acknowledges the limitations under which it must
operate. It now talks in terms of decades to attain goals it saw as only
a few years off a short time ago.

Under these conditions, the Chinese need badly to expand their trade
with the outside world. Trade on a large scale, or of an essentially
different character than that of the present, is hardly feasible or even
desired by the regime. But great benefit would flow from the sale of
more of what China *can* produce in order to buy more of what it critically needs. As the economy is now operating, and seems likely to
continue for the indefinite future, the margin between success and deep
trouble is very thin. The $350 million of exchange earned in trade with

Hong Kong makes, for example, a world of difference. So too with the grain procured from Canada, and the fertilizer from Japan.

Beginning in 1965 and increasingly thereafter, China will be seeking markets for the goods—primarily cotton and silk textiles, food items, and raw materials—previously shipped to the USSR to liquidate its debt to Moscow. Success in this endeavor would also make a great difference. Although less than $300 million of exports would be involved, an increase in China's ability to buy in the West by even this amount would add greatly, perhaps decisively, to the cushion of goods the regime must have to keep the country, and its own power, on even keel.

It is this one point that needs to be most emphasized about Communist China as it is now operating: that is, the key importance of "thin margins." If the regime had persevered in its efforts to transform China into a modernized great power, resources at an astronomical level would have been required. But with the regime willing to forego a program of "socialist construction" for the indefinite future, it can, like other tyrannical regimes of the past, not only maintain a strangle hold on the country but also, because of the sheer size and energy of the population it commands, marshal strength far disproportionate to that of any of its immediate neighbors, *provided* it is able to keep the economy functioning at a "survival level." And very little can go far in this particular.

2. *With little more to go on than its disciplined mastery of three quarters of a billion people, the regime feels able to continue its full commitment to the communist cause.* It quite evidently reasons that if it can but retain its own power intact and keep the economy from breaking down it can pursue its international objectives both actively and effectively even though lacking a "great power" base at home. Here the point again needs to be noted that the regime is thinking in terms of using a "guerrilla strategy" on a world scale. While possessing only a primitive power base it succeeded in inflicting defeat on the Nationalist Government backed by the resources of the United States. Why can not the United States—and the Soviet Union too for that matter—be defeated in the same way? All that had been required in the case of the Nationalists was an effective organization—essentially a military-type organization embracing all society—plus the magical insights of Marxism-Leninism-Stalinism as extended and brought to perfection by Mao? Why should more be required for the United States?

In communist terminology, the Chinese, despite their strident denials, are operating on the basis of "permanent revolution." They see great power capabilities for themselves as the *product* of successful revolutionary struggle, not the reverse. In this they are the heirs of those among the early Bolsheviks of the USSR who saw no chance for victory for the revolutionary cause embodied in the Soviets unless added revolutionary conflicts were generated on an ever extending scale. This contrasts, of course, with the line that triumphed in the Soviet Union; the line adopted by Stalin; the line of first "building socialism in one country."

Under this line, the Soviets concentrated their energies on building a power base that could be brought to bear when and as special opportunities offered for new revolutionary advances (which Stalin at least expected to come only with major international wars in which the USSR itself might or might not be engaged). The Soviets invested their resources to build greater and greater basic strength for future use. The Chinese invest theirs to maximize and get immediate benefit from strength in being, which consists principally of the disciplined masses of the country. They seek to *win* first, and then to build on the basis of their winnings; the Soviets sought to build in order to win. The Chinese way is obviously the more economical—if it works. It is, moreover, the only way open to the Chinese since they do not have and have no prospect of acquiring the resources necessary for a "build first" approach.

3. *Peking still must have not only enough to keep the country running but also weapons that will enable its armed forces to compete under modern conditions of warfare.* While existing industries can supply the small arms and artillery required for a multi-million man army, they cannot supply the sophisticated equipment that even a China has to have to keep pace militarily. At one time, the Soviet Union, albeit reluctantly, helped fill the gap. Most of its assistance was in the form of finished products (radar equipment, self-propelled artillery, a few submarines, anti-aircraft guns, ground control stations, planes and related equipment, etc.) but it also helped to get a few advanced industries started. Since about 1961 the Soviets have halted all military assistance to Peking. As a consequence, the Chinese are now in a relatively desperate situation with regard to advanced weapons. Their military aircraft are approaching obsolescence and increasing cannibalization is necessary to keep these operational; grave deficiencies exist in the radar net; they lack surface-to-air missiles, something even the Indonesians have; they have virtually no mechanized forces and even trucks suitable for military purposes are severely limited; amphibious capabilities are primitive; and naval capabilities worthy of the name hardly exist. Only by drawing on the Free World can Peking overcome shortcomings in its military establishments. It must either import needed weapons and equipment

directly, or it must import machinery and know-how with which to make them itself.

4. *Any possibility China has to achieve a real nuclear capability is particularly dependent on outside help.* The USSR gave the Chinese a start in the nuclear business, although it stopped short of giving them a nuclear weapon or giving them direct assistance in developing an ability to make their own. Peking has proved able to build on the base the Soviets did furnish and to produce and explode two nuclear devices, although a much longer period of time was required than most observers expected. For the regime to go on from this point and attain the status of a "nuclear power" will require infinitely greater resources and more sophisticated equipment and know-how than needed up to now. It can be taken as virtually certain that the USSR will not reverse itself and lend a hand. If, therefore, China is to enter the nuclear club, it will have to ride in on the backs of one or more of the industrialized nations of the free world.

The Sum of the Trade Issue in the Case of China

The failure of the communist regime to make progress toward its "socialist construction" goals has severely limited the potential of China to menace the security of the U. S. and the Free World generally, although it has not eliminated the threat China poses to U. S. and the Free World positions in areas bordering on China itself;

The inability of China to trade freely with the Free World was one of the factors, although of uncertain weight, responsible for this failure;

With the break between Peking and Moscow any future barriers to China's trade with the Free World will bear heavily on Peking and add to the already near insuperable obstacles that stand in the way of the internal development of the country;

The barriers can also importantly limit China's ability to exert military pressures on Free World positions in its immediate environs;

The barriers if shared in by the Free World generally could largely rule out the possibility of China's becoming a nuclear power in any meaningful sense of that term;

The greater the degree of Free World cooperation in the imposition of barriers, the greater will be the effect on China; but unanimity within the Free World is not a requisite for usefulness for the policy; the situation of China being what it is, significant results can be produced by a few countries, and even by the U. S. alone.

While we cannot be sure how much our trade and other policies toward China contributed to the present trend in that country, we can be sure that the trend is in a direction we had hoped it would be when we adopted the policies and that, for the future, the policies can not but strengthen the trend. This strongly suggests that, regardless of the particular turns coming events may take, we should sit tight with the package we now have.

Chapter Thirty

A NOTE ON CUBA

The Overriding Considerations

The U. S. embargo on trade with Communist Cuba is a political necessity. This follows, not from what is happening in Cuba per se, but from the fact that Cuba is a main focal point in the communist struggle against the U. S. and for domination of the Americas.

Cuba represents a penetration of this hemisphere by an alien and hostile system. The object of being of its ruling regime is enmity toward the United States and harm to it and all others in the hemisphere who share the outlook and purposes of the United States. It fosters and supports attacks on the governments of its neighbors. Its ultimate aim is to precipitate and lead a revolutionary holocaust in the Americas.

A Dagger in Hostile Hands: Cuba is part and parcel of the world communist system. It is an avowed and accepted member of the Communist Camp—of the "Socialist Community of States," as Moscow likes to put it. Representatives of the Castro regime—the Cuban *government* in effect—sit in the inner councils of world communist conclaves. Official Cuban representatives actively joined in the debates and shared in the decisions that led to the December, 1960 Moscow "Statement of Eighty-one Parties," which sought to set a strategy for the final victory of the world revolutionary cause. The "victory in Cuba" of itself generated a wave of renewed confidence in world communist ranks, and the continued survival of the communist regime in Cuba adds constantly to that confidence, and particularly among communists and near communists in Latin America. For the western hemisphere, Cuba has given new and grave meaning to the expression "international communist conspiracy."

Cuba is a responsive instrument of Soviet policy in both its anti-U. S. and world revolutionary designs. Its armed forces are under Soviet tutelage, and it serves as a Soviet military base. Castro at one time explained his acceptance of Soviet offensive missiles in Cuba in terms of yielding to a Moscow appeal to strengthen "socialist forces" against their "enemies." Cuba is demonstrating a willingness for "economic integration" and a "division of labor" within the Soviet bloc that exceeds that of any other of the satellites, and this despite its being assigned the traditional colonialist role of agricultural and raw materials producer, a role Rumania rejects and Bulgaria chafes over. Cuba is a ready and willing —in fact an eager—springboard for any activity the USSR wants or may come to want to pursue in the Americas. This willingness to serve the Soviet Union extends over the entire spectrum of Soviet interests and purposes, including the promotion of new Soviet political relationships with Latin American governments, serving as a center for the dissemination of propaganda, providing training for prospective guerrilla fighters, infiltrating espionage agents and trouble makers, arming and supplying insurgents, promoting and managing insurrections, etc.; and should the Soviets wish, it would admittedly extend to helping with an armed attack on the U. S.

The menace Cuba represents for the United States and the Americas flows principally from the fact that it is an integral part of the communist world. Without its ties with the Soviet Union, Castro's Cuba might conceivably fall into the "disagreeable nuisance" category where some observers place it. But with those ties it is an element in the Soviet power structure and a key factor in the communist struggle against the United States.

Cuba to be sure is not simply a carbon copy of other communist states. No communist state is a carbon copy of another. Also, Castro certainly has aims and plans that go beyond the "made in Moscow" stamp. Neither of these circumstances, however, alters or diminishes Cuba's role as an extension of both the Soviet system and Soviet power into the midst of the American Republics, to the very doorsteps of the United States itself. As a matter of fact, Castro's ability to be otherwise minded and to get away with it carries the danger of this role into an added dimension, in that it opens the possibility of the USSR being dragged into an adventure it might not otherwise undertake. In an age given to more realism than our own in the choice of political language, Communist Cuba could hardly fail of characterization as a dagger aimed at the heart of the United States. In a real sense the mere existence of the communist regime in that country represents an act of continuing aggression against the United States and the other American Republics, and first and foremost by the USSR.

Focus on Soviet Ties: The United States has generally failed to face up to this hard reality. The one major exception was during the missile crisis when the U. S. refused to focus on Havana and concentrated attention squarely on Moscow where the responsibility obviously rested. But this *was* an exception. Ordinarily, Castro's Cuba is treated as if it existed in a vacuum, as if it were separable from the rest of the communist world. Witness, for example, the evaluation given by Secretary of State Rusk in the February 1964 address cited above:

> "On our doorstep another communist regime incites and supports subversion, terror and guerrilla warfare against its Caribbean neighbors. More than two years ago the Organization of American States unanimously declared this regime to be incompatible with the inter-American system. The OAS has taken various steps to isolate Castro's Cuba and to curb its capacity to do harm.... There will be no retreat from our policy toward the Castro regime in Cuba as long as it continues to threaten the security and stability of other nations in this hemisphere. Moreover we regard this regime as temporary. With the other nations of this hemisphere, we expect the Cuban people to regain their freedom and rejoin the inter-American system.... The free nations who sell to Cuba goods and equipment important to the Cuban economy are interfering with the efforts of the free nations of this hemisphere to curb this danger. In the missile crisis of 1962 it was evident that what happened in Cuba could directly affect the security of the entire free world. That is still so."

This statement is excellent as far as it goes. But it passes over the all important matter of the relationship between Communist Cuba and the Soviets. It suggests that if the Castro regime would but change its own conduct, U. S. policies toward Cuba might also change, and this without regard to whether Cuba continued as an instrument of Soviet power and an ardent supporter of the Soviet design against the United States and its security.

The Consequences of an Accommodation: An accommodation with Castro without a severance of Cuban ties with the USSR and the rest of the communist world would by definition constitute U. S. acceptance of the permanency of those ties. Granted, the U. S. has in practice made such an adjustment with regard to the countries of Eastern Europe. But if the considerations that have over the centuries governed the efforts of great powers to preserve themselves mean anything, it would seem obvious that Cuba must be viewed by the United States in an entirely different light than the countries of Eastern Europe. And, aside from direct security factors, the responsibilities the United States has willingly borne for fourteen decades as leader of the western hemisphere would seem to make unthinkable a U. S. accommodation to the Cuban regime as long as its communist ties endure.

116

Concrete Results of the Embargo

The trade embargo is, of course, the pivotal element in the U. S. "no-accommodation" policy. Even if the embargo yielded little in the way of concrete results it would have to be continued unless the whole policy is to collapse. The embargo, however, has demonstrably been quite effective. While many factors have contributed to the steady economic deterioration in Cuba since the communist takeover, certainly the denial of trade enforced by the United States, most of the other American Republics, and a substantial part of the Free World at large has played a major part. And for the future the continued isolation of Cuba from its natural trading partners can play an important part in keeping the Cuban problem under at least a degree of control.

An Aid, Not a Solution: It is beside the point that we cannot expect the embargo by itself to bring a collapse of the Castro regime. Some observers appear to harbor and bet heavily on this expectation, while others despair of it and in doing so see little merit in continuing with the embargo effort. But to take either position is to misjudge what the embargo is about, or at least should be about.

Revolutionary movements such as Castro commands are seldom wrecked by the economic deterioration they invariably bring in their wake. Cuba has endured much in consequence of Castro. There is no reason why it cannot endure even more without breaking under the strain, *provided* certain other factors continue to work in its favor. Surface-wise the most important of these factors is the combination of Castro's charismatic appeal and the totalitarian control system he commands. Much more decisive, however, are: (a) support from the USSR; and (b) the *promise* of great things to come, not alone for Cuba and the Cuban people generally but also and more importantly for Castro's own entourage—the ones on whom he depends for effectiveness in totalitarian rule. The U. S. embargo gets at both of these latter factors.

Placing the Burden on the USSR: Regarding Soviet support, the embargo increases the costs to the USSR and at the same time reduces the effectiveness of what the USSR does. The ideal arrangement for Castro's purposes—and for Moscow's—would have been one wherein Cuba could have reoriented itself economically and politically toward the USSR and the socialist camp while simultaneously maintaining a trade relationship with the U. S. and other western markets that would enable it to trade those of its wares that the socialist countries do not want for the goods the socialist countries cannot provide. Under this arrangement, Soviet support could have been highly selective, opening the possibility of maximal results for minimal efforts. But the closure of western markets—

and principally the U. S.—has thrown the entire burden on the Soviet Union and the other socialist countries. And the Cuban economy and its requirements being what they are, the socialist countries despite their great resources have been unable to meet many key demands. Shipments from the East have been vast and the goods represented varied; nevertheless, they have barely kept the economy going.

Contributing to Frustrations: The promise of great things to come in the way of "socialist construction" has been kept a mere promise, and a more and more distant one at that. This above all else represents the pay-off for the U. S. embargo effort. A spectre that has haunted many U. S. observers is the possibility that Cuba would become a glittering Communist "showcase" in the Americas. President Kennedy, for example, seemed more concerned about the possibility than almost any other aspect of the Cuban problem. He saw no reason why the Soviet Union with its vast resources could not transform a tiny island like Cuba into a gardenland of progress and plenty. And he feared a lasting impact on the attitude of the Cuban people and a great impetus to communism in countries that remain frustrated in their developmental aspirations.

Quite obviously the interests of the United States demand that Cuba become no such showcase. It would be shortsighted in the extreme if the United States itself contributed in any way to that end, or if it failed to do all it could to keep other western nations from contributing to it.

The aim of the United States should be not alone to prevent Communist Cuba from becoming a glowing example to other developing countries. It should be also to disabuse the most ardent of the regime's followers and even the members of the regime itself. Lacking, as it seems, an ability to do anything else about communism in Cuba, the U. S. should at the least do everything feasible to make clear that there is no future in it—no future in it for Cuba as a nation, for the Cuban masses, or for the Cuban leaders who would ride communism to positions of personal glory and accomplishment, as well as for the USSR itself or for developing countries that might be tempted to follow Cuba's path.

The Problem and Prospects for the Future

The best ally the U. S. has had in its efforts to build economic pressures in Cuba has been the Castro regime itself. This, however, appears likely to change for the future. In recent months policies that were contributing to the same ends the U. S. embargo is designed to serve have been discarded and the regime has gotten on a course which, unless effectively countered by the United States, may well bring a gradual upturn.

The regime in its first years sought and actively promoted a complete break with the United States. It held as an article of faith the belief that all of Cuba's ills derived from U. S. "imperialist exploitation," and it blanketed under "exploitation" the full range of economic relationships, including regular trade, U. S. investments, tourism, preferential treatment for Cuban sugar imports under the quota system, etc. The tactic of the regime was to avoid formal initiatives on its own part, but to force initiatives by the United States through creating impossible situations, thus fostering the impression of ruthless U. S. pressures on "little Cuba." The regime, however, made no secret of its delight at each step taken by the U. S., hailing even the withdrawal of the sugar quota as a milestone in Cuba's "emancipation" and as an indispensable preliminary to real economic progress.

As rapidly as it could, the regime moved to substitute economic ties with the Soviet Union and the other communist countries for those with the U. S. under which it chafed. And its enthusiasm for the new orientation spilt over and affected Cuba's relationships with other western countries. The pattern of Cuba's trade was suddenly turned upside down, much as had been the case with Communist China ten years earlier. Where in 1959 western countries accounted for 97.8 percent of Cuba's total trade and the communist countries for 2.2 percent, in 1962 the western share was 17.2 and the communist 82.0. Most of the western drop came from the break with the U. S. (the U. S. share of total trade amounted to 69.4 percent in 1959; it was less than one percent in 1962), but a marked decline also took place for other noncommunist countries (from 28.4 in 1959 to 17.2 in 1962).

Meanwhile, and as a concomitant of the trade shift, the regime went all out for "planned socialist construction" and produced an economic shambles in the process. Focus was on "accelerated industrialization" and to the neglect of all other phases of economic life and without regard to Cuba's needs, raw materials situation, labor supply, or ability to pay. Sugar, the mainstay of the economy and almost the sole source of foreign exchange, was made the object of a special "war," the regime viewing the "dominance of sugar" as an enthralling legacy of U. S. "imperialism."

The regime has now swung around full circle. Ambitious industrialization schemes have been thrown out and sugar reinstalled as king. An annual production of ten million tons has been set as a goal for 1970 and Soviet assistance is to be channeled principally into the sugar industry. The stated intention of the regime is not alone to serve as sugar producer for the advanced members of the "socialist camp" but also to reattain a dominant position in the western sugar market and therewith to renew the flow of economic assistance from western countries. Spokesmen acknowledge that for some time increased sugar sales in free world markets can be effected only at a loss. (It costs a minimum of 2.75 cents to produce a pound of raw sugar in Cuba; the September, 1965 price of raw sugar on the world market was 1.8 cents a pound.) They say, however, that Cuba, with Soviet assistance, will absorb the losses in the expectation that within a few years other sugar producing countries will break under the strain, leading to a near Cuban monopoly of the world market.

The new Cuban program adds up to Soviet subsidized economic warfare against other sugar producing countries and through them against the United States, since almost all are closely aligned with the United States. The ultimate aim of course is to make communism work and pay dividends in Cuba in spite of the U. S. embargo. The challenge to the United States would therefore seem clear. And it is a challenge the United States can hardly afford to ignore. To meet it the United States will need not alone to continue its own embargo but also to intensify its efforts to secure cooperation from other western countries. Moreover, the United States will have no choice but to make use of its economic power in other ways to make certain that the Cuban-Soviet gambit does not succeed.

PART 7

GROUNDWORK FOR A STRATEGY

The discussion in the foregoing sections has been designed to highlight the varied and complex factors which need to be taken into account in the decision-making process regarding U. S. East-West trade policy. The concern underlying that exercise was that the trade issue not be treated as if it stood alone, that it be treated in the context of all the circumstances and conditions that will necessarily determine the effectiveness, from the standpoint of U. S. national interests, of any policy decided upon. More specifically, the object has been to establish the framework in which the trade problem must be viewed in terms of the interrelationship between East-West trade policy and the basic national security policy of the United States, the economic factors that bear upon the trade issue, how the USSR looks at the matter of trade with the U. S., and the variety of particular problems and conditions which have special implications for the U. S., which in one way or another bear upon or are affected by U. S. trade policy.

Against this background, what would the U. S. do about East-West trade?

Chapter Thirty-One

THE BASIC QUESTION:
SHOULD U. S. POLICY BE CHANGED ?

Most of the factors that have been discussed weigh heavily against any simple "liberalization" of the U. S. restrictive policy. Why, the question inevitably arises, should the United States relax its trade policy toward the USSR while the USSR still engages the U. S. in a struggle that has as its aim the destruction of the United States; engages it in a cold war contest that, as State Secretary Rusk had said, in Soviet eyes is "for keeps"; and admittedly seeks to use trade as an instrument in that struggle?

As previously suggested, the interrelationship between the trade-restrictive policy and the other policies that enter into the overall strategic design of the U. S. make it undesirable to give up the restrictive policy unless (a) the USSR gives convincing evidence of a genuine intention to abandon its cold war purposes and activities and moves toward the acceptance of standards that are the norm for members of the world community of states, or (b) circumstances indicate that the U. S. can better pursue its strategic purposes through giving up rather than maintaining restrictions.

The Case Against a Relaxation

If these criteria are applied to the situation that currently exists, then a range of factors speak strongly against relaxation at this stage:

1. *No Change in Basic Soviet Policies*: Quite evidently, the USSR is not abandoning its cold war purposes and activities.

2. *Mounting Danger from "Wars of Liberation"*: Rather than easing up in the pursuit of its aggressive aims against the U. S., the USSR is becoming increasingly and more actively embroiled in the "Wars of Liberation" which have as their stated aim forcefully undermining the world position of the U. S. While Communist China has forged into the lead in sparking "Wars-of-Liberation" attacks on the U. S., the USSR because of its unchanged commitments to the world revolutionary cause is, on the one hand, being dragged along in the wake of the Chinese, and, on the other, being led to step up its own direct efforts to destroy U. S. positions in the "intermediate zones" of the world.

3. *Good Results from Present Strategy*: The total of U. S. policies —the overall strategic design the U. S. is following in the struggle that the USSR continues to force on it—appears to be proving effective. And, of course, the restrictive policy is an integral part of the total of these policies, of the overall design. While our strategy is not yielding the quick and absolute results that something in the American character seems always to demand, it is fulfilling the two basic purposes at which it aims: (a) denying to the USSR any fruits from its struggle against the United States; and (b) making sure that the costs of that struggle to the USSR are sufficiently great to make increasingly clear to the Soviet leaders that cold war is not a matter to be engaged in lightly.

4. *Substantial Soviet Economic Gains*: If the U. S. were to lift its restrictive measures, important economic benefits would immediately accrue to the Soviet Union, and its ability to wage cold war would be increased.

a. A measure of the extent and nature of the benefits is the concrete interest that Soviet purchasing agents have shown in U. S. items em-

bodying advanced technology, or otherwise having advantages over commodities available in Western Europe and Japan. The increase in the
volume of goods that would go from the United States to the USSR
would not be very great in absolute terms. But, the usefulness of the
goods for Soviet development, particularly with regard to the new industrial fields which are currently being heavily emphasized, would be
entirely disproportionate to the quantities involved.

b. The economic problems and difficulties to which the Soviet Union
has for some time been increasingly subject (see below) are far too
deepseated for a free flow of commodities from the U. S. to make a
very substantial difference. But U. S. goods would help, particularly
since the industries on which the Soviets are now concentrating are ones
in which the United States holds the leading position.

c. Probably the major economic benefit the USSR would derive from
a change in U. S. trade policy would be the simple entry of the U. S.
into the competition for Soviet markets. Up to the limit imposed by Soviet payment capabilities, American suppliers would doubtless be highly
competitive. This would enable Moscow to exert pressures on the West
Europeans and Japanese. And trends of recent years leave little doubt
that these pressures would work, that they would produce better and better terms for the Soviets. These then could be used as leverage on American suppliers for better terms, opening the possibility of a happy merry-
go-round for the Soviets.

d. If the U. S. should be drawn into a thoroughgoing trade subsidization game in order to meet European competition, the Soviets would of
course be in an enviable position indeed. For U. S. subsidies would
generate counter subsidies on the part of Europeans and Japanese, and
these in turn further subsidies by the U. S.

5. *Significant Soviet Political Gains*: The Soviets would receive impressive political dividends if the U. S. restrictive program were abandoned or substantially modified without a correspondingly important
move on the part of the USSR.

a. The simple fact of the change would constitute a political victory
of some magnitude for Moscow. It would suggest that the U. S. had
been bested in a trial of economic strength with the USSR; that the
United States had simply been unable to do without the Russian market.
The USSR would be receiving a badge of respectability, a status of full
equality in U. S. eyes, that it has long insisted is its right. As a Khrushchev would put it: another blow would have been dealt the U. S. "position of strength policy," and the United States would be making one

more acknowledgment that the days of its world dominance were gone, and that the balance of world forces was shifting ever more strongly in favor of the USSR.

b. From the free world side, the change would necessarily denote a shift in the basic attitude of the U. S., indicating that it had either (a) revised downward its estimate of the seriousness of the Soviet threat, or (b) weakened in its resolve to stand firm against that threat regardless of costs and difficulties. The restrictive policy, perhaps more than anything else, has served to signify United States' concern that all free countries of the world maintain every possible safeguard against the grave dangers engendered by the Soviet-led communist drive; it has given concrete expression to the U. S. contention that the communist countries, by their conduct and policies, have put themselves outside the pale of international respectability; it has symbolized U. S. intention to proceed with the building of a free world community in isolation from the communist bloc. The dropping of the restrictive policy could not fail to have a debilitating impact on the cohesiveness and sense of urgency that the U. S. has been able to build in the free world in the face of the Soviet threat. If the United States, at long last, moved so importantly to accommodate itself to the Soviet regime, without that regime having done anything more than in the past to merit that accommodation, such a step would necessarily undercut the general efforts of the U. S. to marshal free world resources to protect the internal and external frontiers of freedom against communist incursions.

6. *Minimal U. S. Gains*: The direct gains the United States would receive in return for a change in its policy would be modest, to say the least.

a. The U. S. could claim that it was making an important gesture in the interest of promoting world peace, but in doing so it would be admitting that it had been following a policy inimical to peace in the past.

b. Economic benefits to the United States would be marginal at best; they might even be negative unless every safeguard were taken to avoid slipping into subsidization.

c. The often-made point that a relaxation of U. S. policies would lead to better relations with the allies would seem to have little validity. Friction between the United States and its allies over the restrictive policy has come not from what the U. S. itself does but from pressures on the part of the United States to induce the allies to follow tougher policies themselves, plus what many of the allies have considered U. S. interference in their domestic affairs through its efforts to keep subsidiaries of U. S. companies in line and to prevent re-exports of U. S. goods. The elimination of these irritants would no doubt be helpful, but they could be eliminated without the U. S. itself abandoning or substantially modifying its own restrictive efforts. Moreover, U. S. competition in the eastern market, particularly if it involved governmental support, might very well create far more irritants than would have been eliminated.

7.   A balance sheet of pros and cons for dropping U. S. restrictions would thus show a strong case against such a course. It would, in sum, add up to this: without any significant returns for the United States, the USSR would realize significant economic and political gains, while the effectiveness of other U. S. policies toward the USSR and the general ability of the United States to wage cold war would be impaired, perhaps importantly impaired. Moreover, the U. S. would be giving up gratuitously one of the few bargaining counters that it could afford to put on the table in case an opportunity should arise for serious negotiations with the USSR for the settlement of outstanding differences.

Chapter Thirty-Two

A POSSIBLE ALTERNATIVE TO THE PRESENT POLICY: TO USE TRADE AS A POSITIVE INSTRUMENT OF COLD WAR POLICY

The case sketched above presupposes, of course, that the U. S. would simply move from a policy where trade is restricted to one where trade is unrestricted (except for "military items"). There is, however, another possibility: restrictive policy might be replaced by a policy that would allow the United States to use trade, including trade denial, as a flexible instrument in the continuing struggle against the Soviet Union.

To use trade in this manner *effectively,* it should be stressed at the outset, is far easier to talk about than to do. This is true with regard to foreign trade generally, and among all countries, but it is particularly true with regard to trade between the United States and the USSR.

The U. S. can use trade to help the European satellites move toward greater independence, and under certain circumstances that help will be quite substantial. However, the capability of the U. S. to contribute to the process of erosion within the European communist bloc is not dependent upon the abandonment of the restrictive policy, particularly in the case of the USSR itself. As a matter of fact, the effectiveness of U. S. efforts to promote erosion in the relationships among the states within

125

the communist community of Eastern Europe is all the greater because the overall restrictive system does exist. It is this that allows a "differential policy" when and as a communist state gives evidence of a will and capability for greater national independence.

As to the USSR alone, the prospects do not seem good for the United States to accomplish anything of substantial consequence through attempts to use trade as a *direct* instrument of policy. This is partly due to what is almost certain to be a very small volume of trade. It also flows from the fact that the Soviet Union, too, will be trying to use trade to serve its own ends, and that its state monopoly over trade affords it special strength in this regard.

Chapter Thirty-Three

SOME ABSOLUTE LIMITATIONS ON THE U. S.

There are, moreover, several things which, for a variety of reasons peculiar to the USSR, we can be sure the United States cannot do through trade and trade policy vis-a-vis the Soviets:

1. *No Exchange of U. S. Trade Concessions for Soviet Political Concessions.* The Soviets will be more than willing to sit down and negotiate a trade agreement with the United States. But the Soviets would think in terms of negotiating trade and trade-related matters only. The principal thing they would expect to put on the table would be the *promise* of "massive" Soviet orders for American products. Against this, they would want the elimination of U. S. restrictive measures *and* credits —long-term, government-to-government credits. If the U. S. should insist, the Soviets could be expected to sweeten the kitty from their side by agreeing to (a) settlement of U. S. Lend-Lease claims on a "compromise basis"; (b) arrangements for the "mutual" protection of copyrights, patents, and industrial property rights; (c) improvements in consular relations; (d) certain guarantees regarding the treatment of business representatives in each of the two countries; (e) perhaps improved arrangements for cultural exchanges, etc.

If, however, the U. S. in such negotiations should come forward with a proposition calling for the USSR to yield important political positions —say in connection with disarmament; a change in Soviet policies with regard to the U. N.; acceptance of the U. S. position on Berlin or a German settlement; or repudiation of support for "wars of liberation"— the USSR would have none of it. It is not that the Soviets would view an improvement in trade relations with the U. S. as of such marginal importance as to make it not worth bargaining for; actually, as has been said, the Soviets attach great importance to an end to U. S. restrictions and to getting a new trade relationship under way—far greater importance in fact than seems called for by realistic prospects with regard to the volume of trade. The reason the Soviets will not exchange political concessions for trade concessions is that it would run completely against the grain, in a manner of speaking, of the basic position the USSR has been taking with regard to its "right" to trade with the United States. More importantly, the object of the USSR in seeking greater trade with the U. S. is, in the final analysis, to *improve* its political position vis-a-vis the U. S. The Soviets might be willing to go along with a "package" agreement wherein one or more political issues were settled on the basis of "mutual concessions" (i. e. on terms basically acceptable to Moscow) at the same time new trade relations were established. In this circumstance, there might be, in effect, a Soviet yielding on some political point in return for trade favors, provided these favors were of sufficient importance, such as long-term government-to-government credits which the Soviets so badly want, and provided the yielding did not cost the USSR anything very substantial. However, any direct trade-off of political interests as against trade interests seems hardly in the cards.

2. *No Build-Up of a Soviet Vulnerability to U. S. Manipulation of Trade in Support of Political Demands.* The U. S. cannot expect through trade to build up a leverage that could be used against the USSR in the future to get political concessions or to force a change in its conduct. This possibility, it might be noted, has come to have considerable vogue in thinking about the future of East-West trade. The thought is that if the U. S. drops its restrictions and develops a substantial volume of trade with the USSR, the USSR will become increasingly dependent on the U. S. market. Therefore, in a crisis situation, or if the USSR causes difficulties for the U. S. and the West, the U. S. could exert significant pressure on the Soviet leaders by threatening to interrupt trade or actually cutting it off. For example, if, after trade on a regular basis had been reinstituted some time, the Soviets made a move, say, against the western position in Berlin, the U. S., in a threatened or applied trade embargo, would have an important added weapon in its arsenal. The difficulty with this is twofold:

a. The volume of trade for the indefinite future is not likely to be great enough to create any appreciable dependency on the part of the USSR; moreover, the nature of the trade will be such as to make it more important for future *development* than for the satisfaction of current requirements—a circumstance that would make it relatively easy for the USSR to stand up under an interruption of trade, since what would be involved would simply be a delay in fulfillment of plans and not immediately disruptive shortages.

b. But even if the volume of trade should become quite substantial, Soviet policies and conduct over time have made clear that trade and trade relations are expendable commodities in the USSR's conduct of affairs. The Soviet operational methods call for the subordination of trade to political considerations, not the reverse. It might be well to recall both the situation after 1932 and the postwar period when Moscow, at considerable costs, turned its back on trade with the West, particularly with the United States, for political purposes. It might also be well to note that history is replete with instances where the efforts of one nation or a group of nations to use the interruption of trade as a direct weapon in a political or military confrontation have failed. The U. S., which has been prone to rely heavily on the use of trade in this way, has had a dismal record from the standpoint of results. The USSR also, in what appeared to be made-to-order cases for successful application of the tactic, has found it equally unproductive; witness, for example, the failure of the total Bloc embargo on trade with Yugoslavia beginning in 1949, the application of economic sanctions against Albania from 1960, and the Soviet attempt to intimidate the Chinese communists through withdrawing its support of industrialization efforts and severely reordering economic relations in other particulars.

3. *No Change of Heart.* The thought—or hope—that the U. S. can in some way use trade to ease the Soviet regime into a different world outlook and different policies and conduct at home and abroad can also be taken as ill founded, if not out-and-out vain. This point has been stressed in the preceding discussion, and the reasons underlying it set forth in some detail. The point, however, needs to be noted in the context of the matters here being considered, for it not only reflects a very real limitation on what the U. S. can do through a "positive approach" in trade policy, but also puts in perspective one of the often assumed major "costs" of a "hard" policy.

Chapter Thirty-Four

A SPECIAL FACTOR TO BE TAKEN INTO ACCOUNT: THE DEEPENING CRISIS IN SOVIET AFFAIRS

Whether the U. S. has real prospect of making more effective use of trade policy to attain what Secretary Rusk has set as "our transcendent goal: a worldwide victory for freedom" depends on whether a strategy can be devised to capitalize more directly than is now the case on the quiet but deep and many faceted crisis that is increasingly pressing down on the Soviet regime in both its domestic and external affairs. In considering this possibility, however, another and quite different possibility should be kept in mind—that is, we may through a change in our policy inadvertently assist the Soviets in their efforts to escape from this crisis.

It is the crisis itself and the decisive results that may well flow from its prolonged continuation that should loom largest in our thinking and planning about the Soviet Union, and not alone with regard to trade policy. For this crisis stands in importance far above anything else that has occurred since the emergence of the Soviet threat as the main obstacle to a peaceful and orderly world. The crisis has brought the Soviet regime, whether it knows it or not, to a crossroad's point in terms of where it shall go from here; and this is as true of the Kosygin-Brezhnev leadership as it was of the Khrushchev. The main issue at stake for the regime—although the regime itself would be the last to accept this, much less to admit it—is whether the Soviet Union can long continue to serve its deeply rooted commitments to world communism and the goals of world communism without bringing disaster upon itself.

Nature and Extent of the Crisis

What are the main elements and features of this crisis in Soviet affairs?

1. Crisis and Conflict in the Communist Camp

Overshadowing everything else is, of course, the challenge of Communist China to Soviet positions, pretensions, and hopes. The challenge is the focal point of the deep and abiding conflict between the USSR and Communist China that began to unfold in 1956, reached a point of no return between 1959 and 1961, and is now responsible for an unbridgeable and ever widening and deepening chasm between the two erstwhile communist partners. The conflict is rooted in many causes, including a clash of national interests on a wide front; historical and racial antagonisms; personality clashes; highhandedness and arrogance on both sides, coupled with ill concealed mutual contempt; state-to-state clashes and conflicts including repeated border incidents; a different reading of the sacred texts of Marxism-Leninism; differing and mutually irritating operational styles; basic differences in outlook in consequence of varying levels of development; and on and on.

For each side, however, the varied particular causes for the differences and quarreling consolidate into a single overriding and irreconcilable complaint. For the USSR, it is the fact that the Chinese refuse to subordinate themselves and their interests to the will of Moscow, which according to the Leninist-Stalinist book is the first requirement for all good communists, and instead do all they can to undermine the position and influence of the USSR, even as if it were but another "imperialist enemy." For the communist Chinese, it is the refusal of the USSR to expend its wealth and its resources and to risk its national security in support of the world communist cause, which in Peking's eyes has to do primarily with meeting the needs and promoting the ambitions of China.

The challenge of the Chinese has served not alone to create immediate and pressing problems for the Soviets on a variety of fronts; it has also destroyed the basis of the Soviet claim that "with one-third of mankind" in the communist camp, "the balance of world forces has shifted irrevocably in favor of the USSR." More fundamental, the defection of China brought for the first time into sharp focus the basic incompatibility between Soviet national interests and the requirements arising from Soviet commitments to the world communist movement. Previously, this incompatibility had been disguised by the fact that every extension of communism had appeared to be an extension of the power of the Soviet Union itself, since communists everywhere, whether they held state power or not, were subject to Moscow's control and responsive to Soviet interests and policies.

From the standpoint of direct consequences, the Chinese challenge has served to face the USSR with the necessity of either accepting a fundamental and lasting setback in its world position, or coming up with a success or triumph at home or abroad of such magnitude as to reestablish Soviet ascendancy over the Chinese communists and successfully to reassert its primacy in the communist world. Soviet leaders quite clearly do not intend to let the Chinese communists succeed in their efforts to undermine Soviet positions; in consequence they are seeking to offset Chinese pretensions and criticisms by getting themselves far out in front again.

This was a consideration that importantly influenced the ill-fated Cuban missile venture; it is a consideration which also causes the Soviets to overreach their capabilities and to get themselves dangerously involved in revolutionary adventures in the former colonial countries, in trying to influence through trade and aid neutral countries, in maintaining positions and carrying on activities vis-a-vis the U. S. that hold out little prospect of dividends for the USSR. The Chinese problem is also responsible for added urgency in Soviet efforts to cope with internal problems, and to get on with the fulfillment of development plans. In general, then, the conflict with China bears heavily upon and intensifies what, as will be seen, is the most basic element in the crisis situation confronting the Soviet leadership: the growing resources pinch.

Paralleling the conflict between the USSR and Communist China, and interacting with that conflict, is a deterioration of unity and cohesiveness within the satellite states of Eastern Europe. This element in the Soviet crisis reenforces and adds to the enervating consequences of the more important conflict with China. In addition, it has special consequences for the Soviet economic and resources situation. For years, the USSR secured substantial direct benefit from its control over the European satellites. Now the flow is increasingly in the reverse direction. Meanwhile, the Soviet Union's long-cherished hope of integrating the satellite economies into the Soviet economy, with a division of labor arrangement that would have well served Soviet interest, has been all but dashed. Not one of the satellites—with the possible exception of East Germany, where special considerations operate—shows any enthusiasm for the loudly touted Soviet plans, except for such portions as promise that the greater benefit will accrue to it.

The conflict between the USSR and Communist China has shattered the monolithic character of the world communist movement. Moscow, instead of being able, as in the past, to secure conformance to its policies, finds itself faced with the necessity of constantly battling, often without success, to prevent local communist parties and communist-front organizations and groupings from coming under the direct control of the Chinese enemy. Where once the USSR had a sure instrument of policy in the world communist movement, it now has a problem which adds to the strains and difficulties of an already sorely pressed apparatus in Moscow.

2. Growing Commitments and Declining Returns in the International Sphere

The conflict which the USSR has chosen to wage against the United States is a costly affair for both countries. It has kept the USSR under the burden of a terribly expensive arms race, which space explorations have extended into a new and seemingly limitless dimension. It has required the USSR to pour human and material resources it can ill afford to spare into a contest for the developing areas of the world. It has laid on the USSR special costs and harsh burdens in connection with the crises that Moscow has seen fit periodically to interject into the conflict, such as Berlin and Cuba. It has required the expenditure of resources to support communist Cuba, to keep turmoil going in the Congo, to help, to a degree at least, with the communist war against U. S. positions in Southeast Asia.

For more than a decade, the efforts and resources the Soviet Union has expended in its worldwide contest with the United States have yielded very few dividends. Cuba represents, in fact, the only tangible gain the Soviet Union has realized over the past fifteen years. None of the former colonial countries has fallen under Soviet sway; the neutral countries, in which the USSR has made relatively huge outlays, have in a number of cases rewarded Soviet efforts by an assertive anti-Americanism, but at the same time they have avoided any subservience to the USSR. Neither have the crises that the Soviet Union has from time to time generated brought gains for the USSR. As a matter of fact, in the case of the two principal ones—the protracted crisis over Berlin and the sharp but dangerous Cuban missile crisis—the Soviet Union had to back down at considerable cost to its prestige.

Meanwhile, Western Europe has waxed prosperous as has Japan; the United States has moved from one economic high point to another; a number of Latin American countries have begun at long last to move toward their long-held aspirations to modernize; and a number of festering sores within the noncommunist world have been brought under control, if not cleared up. While important frictions have appeared in the NATO alliance, USSR can hardly claim credit for them. In fact, a principal contributing cause has been the loss of momentum in the Soviet Union's outward thrust, and the resultant dulling of the sense of danger in western ranks. And, of course, the difficulties being encountered in the U. S. alliance system pale in comparison with the disarray in the Soviet camp.

Perhaps most significantly of all, the Soviets have not succeeded, either through adventurism abroad or through intense concentration on the arms-space race, in altering the balance of strategic power in their favor. They remain now as at the beginning of the fifties under the shadow of a U. S. strategic superiority that gives the U. S. a sure advantage in any trial of nerves.

3. On the Economic Front

The most critical aspect of the crisis situation within the USSR relates to the economy. This is not by way of saying that the economic structure of the USSR is about to collapse. When taken as a whole, the economic structure is stronger than at any time in the past. Also, progress continues to be made in virtually all fields.

The problem with regard to the economy is that it is not measuring up to the demands which the regime's commitments at home and abroad place upon it. A few main points will serve to underscore the situation.

a. *Slowing Rate of Growth*: The rate of growth of the economy is slowing down at the very time that the rate demands on its product is increasing. While statistical difficulties make impossible anything more than a rough approximation of growth in the USSR, it is clear that after reaching a postwar high in 1958, the rate since then has dropped sharply. In the six years between 1959 through 1964 the annual average was in the neighborhood of only 3 percent, a figure comparable to the long-time trend in the United States. While the decline has been uneven, with some years producing a sudden upward spurt and others a pace well under the average of 3 percent, it can be said with assurance that growth is leveling off at a rate under 5 percent, with the chances that it will be nearer 4 percent than 5.

While such a rate is obviously quite respectable for a major industrial power, it is inadequate for the attainment of the firmly established goals of the leadership. For example, it will not make possible the cherished and highly touted aim of overtaking the United States in per capita production. It will not, as a matter of fact, make possible in the foreseeable future overtaking the United States in terms of absolute production. For, the laws of arithmetic being what they are, the spread between U. S. production and Soviet production continues to grow. For example, in 1964 the gap equalled $330 billion, which compared with one of $191 billion in 1956. While Soviet growth is adequate to insure a steady but small improvement in living standards, it cannot possibly bring about that state of abundance which the Soviets consider necessary to realize the conditions for a "communist society."

b. *Resources Allocation Problem:* The combination of a slowing growth rate and an expanding body of requirements has produced an acute resources pinch. As the Soviet leaders themselves have openly acknowledged, the USSR simply does not have enough in the way of resources to do all of the things it is trying to do, much less all it needs to do or wants to do. The major reasons for mounting requirements are the efforts of the regime to keep pace with the United States in the arms-space race and the perennial drive to expand the heavy industry base. Well over two-thirds of total production in the USSR goes into these two sectors, which account for an ever-increasing percentage of the annual increment in production. At the same time the regime is ably scrounging for resources needed to expand as rapidly as possible the power base; it is trying to make progress against the chronic agri-

133

cultural problem; it is moving to expand housing, and to get some improvement in the consumer goods sector. And, of course, there continues the large requirements related to Soviet commitment abroad and the increasing pressures generated by the contest with Communist China.

c. *Malfunctioning of Economic Control and Management:* A growing crisis exists in the field of management. The Soviet economy has long been too large and too complex to be efficiently managed on the basis of absolute control from the center, the archaic system of planning, and divided authority between Party bureaucrats and managerial personnel. Complaints from within Soviet ranks have underscored how near to impossible the situation has become in recent years. Khrushchev made something of a career of raving and ranting about managerial shortcomings, and resorted to so-called reform after reform, as well as to repeated personnel upheavals, in the hope of doing something about them.

Publicists have ridiculed the mountains of paper that are required for the operation of a single plant, pointing out that literally tons of documents are required on a continuing basis. One engineer estimated that if things continue as they are, within a relatively few years virtually every inhabitant of the Soviet Union will be required simply to carry on planning work. A different sort of index of the mounting distress over the management system is the publication of plans and expectations in regard to the use of an elaborate national computer complex.

The result of the serious and growing managerial deficiencies is an across-the-board magnification of economic ills. For from these deficiencies flow much of the waste and inefficiency that have always marked the Soviet economy.

d. *Perennial Agricultural Lag:* The chronic agricultural problem seems to get worse rather than better. Some western estimates hold that if current intentions in regard to agriculture are carried out, significant improvement should take place over the next ten or so years. However, implementing these intentions depends upon the availability of resources. If agricultural plans are pushed through regardless of consequences, then almost certainly repercussions will occur in other sectors of the economy. But since the impact would necessarily have to be on the power base sector (that is, on the expansion of heavy industry and the arms-space effort), it is highly questionable that plans will be pushed through in such a manner. Either way, however, agriculture will continue for the indefinite future to be a drag on general economic progress.

e. *Inadequacy of Consumer Goods:* The consumer sector also poses serious problems. The failure of the regime to provide for adequate production of consumer goods in the past has been a major factor in keeping down labor productivity in both industry and agriculture. There simply are not enough consumer items available to make possible adequate incentives for the working force. Consumer industries have never been a forte of the Soviets. Because of the lack of priority treatment and adequate investments, consumer industries have not shared in the modernization process. Soviet capabilities are far under those of the industrialized countries of the West, particularly of the United States. Moreover, to break out of the state of backwardness that has always marked the consumer goods industries, planning, allocation, and priority patterns that are deeply entrenched will have to be broken, something that requires overcoming strong if not immovable resistance. Nevertheless, it can be said with some assurance that only if and as the Soviets do succeed in stepping up their consumer industries and agriculture can other economic deficiencies be overcome.

f. *Tightening Gold Supplies and Growing External Commercial Debts:* While obviously of less import than the foregoing circumstances, the fall in Soviet gold reserves is indicative of the sort of economic pressures that are operating on the regime. As noted above, the Soviets have been forced over the past ten or so years to ship gold at a rate appreciably above production. Reserves have now fallen to under $1.5 billion. For the future, therefore, gold sales will have to be curtailed, reducing the quantity of goods that can be secured from abroad. Meanwhile, the USSR has built up a short and medium-term debt to Western Europe that is now approaching the $1 billion mark; and currently new long-term debts are being added to this.

g. *Some Spot Problems:* Also, the import by the USSR of some $800 million of wheat in 1963-64 remains extremely significant, and reports of disturbances in various parts of the USSR because of a shortage of food supplies cannot be totally discounted. Significance also attaches to the increase in butter and meat prices in 1962, and to the great decline in talk, even on the part of Khrushchev before his fall from power, about plans to overtake the United States in this or that area of production at this or that particular time.

4. Popular Restlessness

Public opinion and popular attitudes have presumably never been weighty factors in Soviet affairs. Certainly, the regime has been able to get away with things over the years that one would never have expected to be tolerable to a people with the revolutionary tradition of the Russians. Yet, since the death of Stalin, there have been strong if subtle evidences that the feelings of the people are not entirely discountable. On the morrow of Stalin's death, the new rulers publicly acknowledged concern to avoid "panic and disarray." And since that day the regime has taken great care to explain and justify to the people its moves and measures. For the most part, the post-Stalin leaders, no more than Stalin himself, do not seem to have let considerations related to public attitudes determine their major decisions and actions. But one startling exception to this might be indicative of a far greater change in the role of public opinion than is recognized on the outside—that is, the purchase of grain from the western market for public consumption.

A step of this nature was without precedent in Soviet history; and it came at a time when the regime was husbanding its resources to procure machinery and equipment abroad necessary to develop critically needed new industries. Why this radical departure from past practices? Why this unusual concern for the welfare of the people? The answer almost certainly does not include the regime's fear of a popular uprising; or fear that disturbances of the type that took place on several occasions over the last few years in connection with food shortages would get out of hand. What worried the regime was a popular vote "by the feet"; that is, one that simply involves dragging the feet.

And this well might be a cause for concern. In agriculture, a major source of the chronic difficulties is the unwillingness of the peasants to strain and sacrifice with so little in the way of rewards for their labors. And as was suggested above, the peasants are not an exception to a general rule, only the most striking example of an altogether general rule.

In recent years the Russian people, including the privileged as well as the masses, have given unmistakable evidence of mounting discontent over the failure to realize their expectations; over the failure of the regime to make good on its commitments to effect a rapid improvement in living standards; over the gap between claims and realities. Disaffection strongly touches the youth, the intelligentsia, and for different reasons the managerial and technical elite. It manifests itself in a "conflict between generations"; in widening protests against bureaucratic mismanagement; in resistance to the dictates of party hacks; and in the growing trend among individuals and groups to escape from a drab and unpromising reality by almost any means available. Apathy and lethargy, not revolution, are likely to be the principal products of the growing dissatisfaction. But given the need of the country to increase productivity, to overcome long-standing and increasingly burdensome deficiencies in the economy and in society generally, given the need "to get moving again," lethargy may be hardly less troublesome to the regime or less decisive in its results than attempts at violence.

5. The Loss of Momentum

It is in the lack of movement toward established goals, both domestic and foreign, that the varied problems and difficulties that now beset the Soviet Union reach their focal point. No reason exists for an expectation that the regime will collapse or be plunged into acts of desperation. Also, the crisis is not, nor is it apt to become, of a nature that would undermine basic Soviet power. The problem is one of frustration—the inability of the regime to do what it wants to do and is committed to do. It is one of drag, of a slowing down, of being unable to break out of binds and to get going again. This loss of momentum for the Soviets, as a dedicated communist regime, is utterly serious. At stake is the dynamics of communism on which the regime's future hopes depend; and at stake also is the more immediate and tangible matter of the relative position of the USSR vs. the United States and its ability to give a convincing answer to the carping attacks of Communist China.

Chapter Thirty-Five

THE SEARCH FOR A WAY OUT

Twists and Turns of a Harassed Leadership

To escape from the binds of the deepening crisis, to regain lost momentum, has been the overriding concern of the Soviet leaders in recent years. An intensive search is on for a way out. Malenkov's premiership following the death of Stalin in April, 1953 began with a frank exposure of accumulated problems and shortcomings, and a flurry of dramatic pronouncements regarding plans for far-reaching "reforms." When it came to specific measures, however, confusion and indecision prevailed. The struggle and conflict within the post-Stalin leadership that led to the fall of Malenkov and the emergence of Khrushchev largely centered on what the remedies should be and how far they should go. And Khrushchev's entire reign was taken up with starts and stops, trials and experiments, movements and reversals, harangues and exhortations, innovations and repudiations, head knocking and chest thumping, reorganizations and re-reorganizations, all designed to reduce the malfunctioning of the system at home and to score successes that would reverse the decline of the USSR in world affairs and restore its dominance over the world communist movement.

137

There were instances of apparent success for Khrushchev's efforts. The "virgin lands" program brought a sudden sharp increase in grain supplies, albeit at great costs. Industrial growth was rapidly accelerated. Living conditions improved substantially. And then came Sputnik and the early space triumphs with their far-reaching impact on both the Soviet image and Soviet confidence. But the basic problems remained. The virgin lands proved a short-lived answer to the chronic difficulties in agriculture; after the spurt from 1954-1958, the rate of economic growth first slowed and then slipped steadily downward; deficiencies in the system of management and control became more and more evident and bothersome; crisis mongering over Berlin and attempts at rocket blackmail proved counter-productive; the Chinese communists moved from veiled criticism to open and vicious attack; and the Russian people responded less and less well to the old techniques of combined exhortations and promises to spur them on to greater efforts and sacrifices.

After 1959-60, a note of desperation increasingly marked Khrushchev's efforts to get things done by stirring things up. He began even to impinge upon the most sacred of the sacred cows within the Soviet Union: entrenched vested interests. Because of this, and because his flailings about were not producing needed results, the *Apparat* of the Communist Party, in which sovereignty in the Soviet Union finally resides, dispensed with Khrushchev and replaced him with a precariously balanced collective leadership. For this new leadership, the great task, the overriding task, remains the same as for Khrushchev: to find a way out of binds and to get the Soviet Union moving again.

The Great Obstacle: Inviolableness of the System

The main difficulty that has stood in the way of a solution to this task has been the unwillingness of the regime, or the inability of the regime, or both—whether headed by a Malenkov, a Khrushchev, or so far a Brezhnev-Kosygin—to touch the Soviet system itself. The regime has, in other words, sought to overcome its problems within limits imposed by the requirement of protecting and preserving the system. Since most of the problems and difficulties which need to be solved are the product of the system, this has had the effect of dooming all efforts to failure. If the system could be changed, the situation would be different; in fact, many of the problems would simply fall away. But without a change in the system, the leaders, whoever they are, can only retread well trodden paths or experiment with what amounts to more of the same. Certainly it was thus with Khrushchev, whose loudly proclaimed "reform programs" were invariably either a rehash of something already tried, or a reversal of an earlier "reform" program that had failed.

The problem adds up to a study in dilemmas:

—The Soviet Union has reached a stage where movement toward established goals both at home and abroad requires either solving a number of basic and increasingly difficult problems or leapfrogging them in such a way that new momentum is made available.

—This puts the present Soviet leadership in a position where it must either (a) continue to struggle in established ways with those problems and difficulties and thus fail, as Khrushchev failed, in its efforts to fulfill its commitments to communism domestically and internationally; or (b) carry through a painful transformation of the very system that has made the Soviet Union what it has been for the past forty-seven years —that is, abandon its commitments to communism; or (c) achieve an increasingly difficult quantum jump, in either a power or economic sense, of such dimensions and significance as to leapfrog the restraints of current problems and weaknesses and generate massive new momentum toward the realization of established goals.

Chapter Thirty-Six

CONCENTRATION ON A BYPASS
OF CRISIS PROBLEMS

Striving for a Leapfrog

The regime, even as it has sought through various devices to "solve" the problems and difficulties of the moment, has consistently staked its main hopes on bypassing rather than eliminating these problems and difficulties. It has aimed at the quantum-jump technique that would simply leave nagging and frustrating problems, difficulties, and weaknesses far behind as it moved forward with its plans. The regime has worked to achieve some sort of signal success to push so far forward in one or another key power sector, or to come up with some new method of doing things on a scale and of a nature that would enable a leapfrog of current restraints —that would, as it were, instantly carry the Soviet Union to an entirely new stage of power or development. This, as previously stated, was the sort of thing that Stalin did with his forced-draft industrialization and collectivization program through "mastering" and exploiting the "weak links" in western positions left as an aftermath of the war, and by his costly but eminently successful drive to modernize Soviet armed forces and to achieve a nuclear and long-range rocket capability.

139

Hopes and Frustrations Regarding an Easy Quick-Fix

The leaders would like to attain their leapfrog in some quick and easy way. Should the opportunity offer they will surely attempt to achieve it through a political or territorial coup, as they evidently hoped to do with Berlin; or through securing a strategic advantage over the U. S. as they sought with missiles in Cuba; or to effect a breakthrough in the space-armaments field, as they almost did with their first-generation ICBM's and Sputnik.

The range of possibilities for an easy quick-fix that would move the USSR into a new power dimension as against the U. S. (and incidentally Communist China) is now, however, extremely narrow. The United States is committed under its present policies to do all it can to deny the Soviets any of the breakout triumphs they seek, whether in the territorial, political, or space-armaments field. Granting continued U. S. firmness in its commitments, it certainly has the capability to frustrate the Soviets along any of these lines.

Willingness to Do It the Hard Way: The regime appears increasingly to recognize and to accept the limitations under which it must operate. While it quite evidently keeps a weather eye for any break or opening that it might seize upon to effect a sudden forward jump, the regime is diligently working toward developing new strengths in selected areas that will serve as a springboard to a new—and the regime hopes supreme—power position.

Chapter Thirty-Seven

THE GOAL: TECHNOLOGICAL PREEMINENCE BASED UPON CAPITALIST EFFICIENCY HARNESSED TO SOCIALIST PURPOSE

As was pointed out previously, the regime sees the attainment of technological preeminence over the United States as the answer to its need. The future, as the Party Program proclaims, lies with advanced technology. If the USSR can achieve unquestioned leadership in science and technology, then, the thought is, it can do all the other things it aspires to do and is committed to do, including the worldwide extension of its system.

How to attain technological preeminence? Not through a burst of individual accomplishments, important though these might be. But through so restructuring and adding to the operational elements in the Soviet system as to enable it to realize the full potential of "socialism" to accomplish what the capitalist system allegedly is incapable of accomplishing, that is: "To effect the scientific and technical revolution . . . on which mankind is now entering . . . bound up with the conquest of nuclear energy, space exploration, the development of chemistry, automation, and other major features of science and engineering."

The leadership is openly seeking ways and means of "releasing the potential" of the system without touching the essentials of the system itself. A massive program is underway that has as its object bringing to bear the full potential of cybernetics on the planning process, and on the administration and management of the economy. The leadership has also taken exploratory and experimental steps toward utilizing elements of a market system within the framework of the existing system of economic planning and control. Perhaps most important of all, there has been the renewed drive to draw, on a highly selective basis, on the knowledge, the experience, and the technological competence of the industrialized West that have made for the far greater efficiency of western economies as compared to the Soviet's.

What the regime is seeking in this last regard has traditionally been called in the Soviet Union "American efficiency." But the USSR wants to secure "American efficiency" without having to accept other elements in the American system, elements that would be dangerous to the Soviet system itself. What it wants, in other words, is to incorporate into the Soviet system American-type methods and over-all technological competence so as to make the Soviet system work better—with safeguards against contagions that might undermine or alter it.

Stalin some forty years ago spelled out the need as it appears still to be seen today, including the need to avoid taking the dangerous with the helpful.

After calling for what he termed a "Leninist style in work," Stalin argued that such a style required "two specific features: (a) revolutionary sweep and (b) American efficiency." He then explained:

"American efficiency . . . is an antidote to 'revolutionary' Manilovism and fantastic improvisation. American efficiency is that indomitable force which neither knows nor recognizes obstacles; which with its business-like perseverance brushes aside all obstacles; which continues at a task once started until it is finished, even if it is a minor task; and without which serious constructive work is inconceivable. But American efficiency has every chance of degenerating into a narrow and unprincipled commercialism if it is not combined with the Russian revolutionary sweep. Who has not heard of that disease of narrow practicality and unprincipled commercialism which has not infrequently caused certain 'Bolsheviks' to degenerate and to abandon the cause of the revolution? We find a reflection of this peculiar disease in a story by B. Pilnyak, entitled *The Barren Years,* which depicts types of Russian 'Bolsheviks' of strong will and practical determination, who function very energetically, but without vision, without knowing 'what it is all about,' and who, therefore, stray from the path of revolutionary work. No one has been more incisive in his ridicule of this disease of narrow commercialism than Lenin. He branded it as 'narrow-minded practicality' and 'brainless commercialism.' He usually contrasted it with vital revolutionary work and the necessity of having revolutionary perspective in all our daily activities, thus emphasizing that this unprincipled commercialism is as repugnant to true Leninism as 'revolutionary' improvisation.

"The combination of the Russian revolutionary sweep with American efficiency is the essence of Leninism in party and state work.

"This combination alone produces the finished type of Leninism worker, the style of Leninism in work."

Chapter Thirty-Eight
IMPLICATIONS FOR U. S. STRATEGY

Given the struggle in which the Soviets engage us, it is obviously in the national interest of the United States that the Soviet Union not succeed in its efforts to effect a quantum jump that would enable it to break out of the binding pressures of its present crisis while still preserving intact the essential features of its system. It is in the national interest that the Soviet Union instead be forced (a) at a minimum, to wrestle more or less hopelessly with its problems and difficulties; or (b) at a maximum, to undergo a transformation of its system. The strategic plan of the United States is, of course, tailored to these requirements; that is, it is designed to deny the Soviet Union a breakout, and to force it to stew in the juices produced by its system—unless and until it comes to a transformation in that system, which among other things is the source of Soviet hostility and aggressiveness toward the United States and the free world.

Role of U. S. Policies in the Growth of Crisis

While many factors have entered into the making of a crisis in the USSR, the policies encompassed in the strategic design of the United States have certainly contributed. The origin of Soviet difficulties obviously lies in the weaknesses of the Soviet system itself and in the fantastically expensive commitments to the cause of communism at home and abroad. But the policies of the United States in association with other free countries have served to make the weaknesses more acute and to increase the costs and burdens of the commitments. And so long as the policies of the U. S. are adhered to, the weaknesses will endure and the costs mount.

What of U. S. trade policy in this situation? We should not exaggerate the direct role played by U. S. trade denial in the growth of crisis in the USSR. Yet, it is easy to conjecture that a different trade relationship between the Soviets and the United States, say such as the one actively sought by the U. S. in the first postwar years, could have made a tremendous difference in Soviet economic development, particularly with regard to the elements that so preoccupy the leadership today: "Achieving the most rational and effective use of material, labor, and financial resources and natural wealth . . . eliminating excessive expenditures and losses . . . achieving the highest results at the lowest cost . . . concentrating on the rapid development and introduction of new techniques. . . ."

Trade with the U. S. as a Possible Factor in Soviet Recovery

Be that as it may, the regime admittedly is looking to increased imports of technologically advanced machinery and equipment and know-how as one of the main means to reverse the present trend and supply new thrust to the Soviet economy, and with that, step up Soviet power generally. The Soviets have easy access to the markets of Western Europe and Japan and much of what they are seeking can be procured there. However, those markets have been open for more than a decade, yet access to them has not enabled the regime to secure the results it wishes and needs. Access to the U. S. market, too, might not make much difference. But then it might. We simply have no way of knowing. We can only speculate as to the margin that would spell the difference in the USSR at this stage between economic doldrums and rapid economic movement.

The matter comes down to whether we want to take a chance on helping the USSR to free itself from a restraint that is importantly limiting its capability to pursue its aggressive purposes against the U. S. and the Free World. Considering the depth of the U. S. commitment to do all it can to keep the USSR under such restraints, it would seem almost axiomatic that we would not want to take that chance, even if it should in fact be quite slim.

The Strategic Requirement on the U. S.: Continued Use of Trade Policy to Induce Change in the Soviet System

Short of a convincing Soviet demonstration of a change of heart, demands of our national security strategy would seem to permit a change in U. S. trade policies toward the USSR only in ways and to the extent that direct pressures would be produced on the basic elements of the Soviet system.

Are there realistic possibilities of such a use of trade and trade policy? An opening may exist, or come to exist, in the Soviet search for efficiency. Let us assume that the Soviet aim is, as Stalin said it should be, to procure American efficiency but under conditions and circumstances that would avoid "narrow and unprincipled commercialism" as a by-product—that is, to avoid consequences in the ways of individual enterprise that would be inimical to the Soviet system. If this is so, the United States might set as its aim to let the USSR have access to American efficiency—in the form of the products and the knowledge and the technological competence that are the fruits of the American economic system—but *only* under conditions and circumstances that would make reasonably certain that the procurement would produce as a by-product just such a "narrow and unprincipled commercialism" as the Soviets want so desperately to avoid.

A Significant Trend on which to Target?

A concrete basis on which the U. S. might build, or in Stalinist terms a "weak link" that the U. S. might seize upon, may already exist. This relates to the cautious exploration of introducing elements of a market system into Soviet economic planning and management. While, as noted above, the regime has sought to keep those explorations within extremely narrow limits, the need for a thorough overhaul of established practices has become so pressing that it has permitted the airing of ideas that could lead to very basic changes. Not only that. The regime has itself instituted pilot programs to test some of these ideas in recent months, on a fairly impressive scale. What has happened to communist thinking and where it may go in the future are indicated in a *Pravda* account of June 22, 1965, of an "Economic Conference" at Moscow University where "representatives of thirty Soviet towns debated keenly for four days."

> "All the discussion revolved in the main about three questions: how to provide a scientific basis for planning and production control, how to bring all economic levers into action, and how to improve the system of material stimulation.

> "Under socialism the use of economic laws is only possible through a plan, the role of conscious adjustment of public production, but such a role can only be fulfilled by a plan which is based on the conclusions of science and practice and which correctly reflects the requirements of society.

"Economists pointed out that the time has come to end detailed planning from above, to cut down the number of indices approved for works, and thereby to create conditions for operative independence and the development of healthy economic initiative of undertakings. In the opinion of many economists, profits should become the basic source of the formation of funds of undertakings, to be spent on the material encouragement of workers. Means for the development of production and the carrying out of social and cultural measures should come from profits. Before profits can be brought into economic practice however, as a basic index, prices must be put in order.

"Much was said about the improvement of wages. It is expedient to increase the part of bonus payments in wages in order to increase the interest of each worker in the results of the activities of undertakings.

"Participants in the conference spoke about the problem of studying and using the internal market. For a long time it was maintained in economic literature that the problems of the market do not exist under socialism. Life has refuted this dogmatic point of view. It is not possible to answer questions about the structure of industry and the organization of production or to determine the trend of industrial development without knowing the volume and demands of the market and the regular laws and prospects of its development. The market problem exists not only for consumer goods but also for the means of production."

What Would be Required of the U. S.?

How might the U. S. exert influence? The key would be for the U. S. to require the USSR to pay for American goods either in cash or with commodities that can find a ready market in the United States. This would exclude the use of credits, except for commercial credits, in the usual meaning of that term, which are necessary for the orderly conduct of foreign trade transactions. It would also exclude special efforts on the part of the United States, or within the United States, to develop markets for traditional Soviet exports, that is, petroleum, crude materials, wood and wood products, and low-quality manufactures. Such products would not need to be excluded. But they should be taken only if markets for them exist without special promotional activities.

What the United States would be requiring through such a control of trade with the USSR would be that insofar as the Soviets desired to trade with the United States they would trade under the same conditions that normally exist between trading partners—that is, each would come forward with goods that are useful to and desired by the other. The effect of this requirement would be the development of export industries by the USSR, if and to the extent that it wished to trade with the United States.

Of course, the USSR might well choose under this circumstance not to carry on trade with the United States in any substantial quantities. If so, this choice should not disturb the U. S.; the U. S. should accept it and not attempt to stimulate increased exchanges. What would be happening in this case would be the enforcement by the Soviet Union of a trade denial policy on itself; the Soviet Union would be denying itself the technological help it clearly desires from the United States.

If, on the other hand, the Soviet Union chose to develop the export capabilities necessary for substantial trade with the U. S. the consequence would be a directly proportionate encouragement of those trends in the Soviet Union that are making for the "unprincipled commercialism" that so worried Stalin. Export industries on any substantial scale would not fit into the scheme of things dictated by the requirements of the Soviet system. Thus, for the development of export industries, adjustments in the Soviet system itself would be required. And these adjustments, even though probably relatively small in scope, could not help but add weight to the forces that are already working for a breakdown of the rigidly controlled economy of the USSR. They would involve getting into a new dimension of experimentation with the principles of a market economy, a dimension wherein the whim of Soviet controllers would be unable to prevail.

In this way, and very probably only in this way, can the U. S. hope to influence directly the choice of alternatives by the Soviet leaders as they carry on their desperate efforts to break out of the binds and restraints that are now pressing in on them.

In this way, also, the U. S. will reduce the risk of contributing to an escape of the Soviet regime from the reckoning that history appears in the process of preparing for its unnatural and meaningless campaign against mankind in the name of communism. The great hope the United States has for a final resolution of the conflict in which the USSR has engaged it lies in the possibility that the weight and costs of Soviet commitments to communist goals will bring the regime to shed those commitments, in fact if not in words. The quiet but very real crisis now engulfing the Soviet world furnishes solid ground for this hope. The greatest concern of the U. S. should be that this crisis runs full course. The aim of the U. S. trade policy, as also for other policies, must therefore be to contribute to the workings of that crisis toward basic changes in the USSR. To this end, trade between the U. S. and the USSR should either be held to a minimum as is now the case or so managed and controlled as to deny the regime any free ride at the expense of the U. S. and to insure that the USSR pays for what it gets, regardless of how much or how little that may be, through adjustments in the Soviet system, even if those adjustments are minor.

Chapter Thirty-Nine

HOW THE U. S. WOULD NEED TO PROCEED

The Requirement for Caution

In any effort the United States might make to use trade and trade policy to induce changes in the Soviet system, it will have to contend with and safeguard against two circumstances that would be working toward counter purposes:

1. The Soviet regime, as previously stressed, would be alert and elusive. To bait a trap for the Soviets is one thing; to catch them in it is another. The regime wants greater trade with the U. S.; but it wants greater trade in order to strengthen its system, make it work better, and otherwise improve Soviet prospects for attaining long established goals. It has always been predictable that Moscow would read any U. S. initiative to improve trade relations as a sign of weakness, as proof of the correctness of its view that the need for ever-expanding foreign trade constitutes a special U. S. vulnerability; it is also predictable that it would attempt to turn the initiative to its own advantage, to use it to get the sort of trade terms that would serve its own interests. A case in point, and one that should be quite sobering, is the reaction of *Izvestiya,* the official organ of the Soviet Government, to the April, 1965 *Report* of the special committee appointed by the President of the United States to study U. S. trade relations with the East European countries and the Soviet Union (the "Miller Committee Report"). An Izvestiya Commentary of May 13, 1965, had this to say:

> "The report of the special presidential commission on trade relations of the United States with the Soviet Union and other socialist countries of East Europe has been published in Washington.

> "The growth and strengthening of the economic power of the socialist countries cannot but exert influence on the attitude of large American business toward trade with the socialist countries. Obviously this is the reason why the report reveals a more realistic approach to the appraisal of the prospects for world trade and the role played in it by the countries of the socialist camp. The captains of American business are beginning to grasp the fact that the old policy of refusing to trade with the USSR and the other socialist countries has not justified itself.

> "Having said 'A' however, the authors of the report do not say 'B.' Instead of drawing the logical conclusion that it is necessary to develop mutually advantageous equal relations in trading with socialist

countries, they engage in dealing with this question from the point of view of U. S. foreign policy aims. And here it becomes obvious that the atmosphere of anticommunist hysteria—which has been energetically pushed by the Pentagon since the beginning of the overt aggression in Vietnam—has clearly affected the recommendations contained in the report. The authors of this report openly declare that foreign trade must be subordinated to the general strategy of the 'struggle against communism.'

"Restriction of trade in so-called strategic goods, the list of which actually includes purely peaceable goods, refusal to grant long-term credits to socialist countries, investing the U. S. President with the right to grant as he sees fit the status of most-favored-nation to individual socialist countries: such are the types of recommendations contained in the report.

"All this, of course, has nothing in common with sincere solicitude for the development of trade. The attempts of the U. S. ruling circles to make the expansion of trade dependent on certain conditions and to develop economic relations with certain states of the socialist camp, while at the same time engaging in aggression against others and striving to sneak in rotten ideological goods under the banner of expanding trade and cultural contacts, are doomed beforehand to failure."

2.   Foreign trade, once under way, has a way of generating its own dynamics. This is particularly true for the United States with its tradition of private initiative and competitiveness. Purposeful use of trade as an instrument of policy therefore is sure to be a tricky and difficult business. While acceptance of a categoric injunction, particularly in terms of national security requirements, is in keeping with American respect for law, trade manipulation by government decision can be something else again. This bespeaks a bureaucratic encroachment on the free enterprise system. Furthermore, it is already apparent that momentum is gathering behind the idea that greater and greater trade between the United States and the European communists, including the Soviets, will in itself serve the national interest.

An assumption that the U. S. can protect and promote its interests by establishing a general set of conditions under which trade with the East European communists is to operate, and then relying upon the workings of the market place to achieve results satisfactory to the U. S. in the way of volume and content and conditions of trade is hardly a safe assumption. The market place when left alone makes its own rules, rules that aim at trade for its own sake, at the maximum level, and of any content that economic factors make feasible.

A prerequisite for an effective use of trade as an instrument of policy against the communist countries is that the U. S. not simply end or liberalize its present control system but that it replace it with another. And this substitute system must provide for flexibility on the part of the U. S. to make quick changes in the course and content of trade if and as political considerations dictate. A second prerequisite is that trade between the U. S. and the USSR be within the framework of a bilateral agreement that would cover both the general conditions of trade and commodity exchanges. How might the U. S. proceed with these requirements in mind?

What to Do and How Far to Go?

The U. S. can move to replace its present control system with a new system in either of several ways:

1. *The Administrative Route:* The President might use the discretionary authority granted him under existing legislation to change the criteria for licensing exports to communist countries, with Johnson Act restrictions on private credit left intact and denial of Most-Favored-Nation treatment for imports from communist countries continued. This is essentially the route the U. S. took in 1964 with Rumania. It would have the advantage of being the easiest and quickest to effect. It would have the further advantage of being reversible at any time political considerations demanded. However, it would offer a poor basis on which to negotiate an agreement with the USSR on terms desired by the U. S. The USSR while attempting to secure benefit from changes in U. S. licensing practices would complain bitterly of continued "discrimination" in regard to the denial of MFN, credit limitations, etc. And the U. S. would be unable to exert pressures on the Soviets to expand their export capabilities because of an inability to set import quotas in either quantitative terms or by categories of goods. Also, continued denial of MFN would constitute a barrier to the sale of products of new Soviet export industries in the U. S. market.

2. *The Legislative Route:* The Congress might repeat or substantially amend one or more or all of the legislative acts on which the restrictive system is based; or it might substitute for those acts one or more new acts which would provide for a mandatory change in the system along certain lines. But this would have the major defect of not providing the flexibility that is essential if trade is to be used as an effective instrument of policy.

3. *The Combined Legislative-Administrative Route:* The Congress might amend existing legislation to extend the President's discretionary authority into areas where it is now lacking, thus allowing him to grant

149

Most-Favored-Nation treatment to the communist countries at his discretion, and to suspend application of other restrictive measures. (This is the course that has been followed with Yugoslavia and in part with Poland.) The President would then have the authority to use or not use any part of the restrictive system that he saw fit. The Congress as an alternative might substitute for existing acts a new comprehensive act under which the President would be allowed a greater or lesser degree of discretionary authority.

A new, single act in which a legislative framework for a comprehensive control system was preserved, but which granted the President virtually full discretionary authority would probably best meet "instrument of policy" requirements. It would enable the introduction into the control system of added elements and refinements that are needed for policy effectiveness. It would also be a far more orderly way in which to proceed.

What Should a New All-Embracing East-West Act Provide?

The act, which for reasons of tact might be entitled "An Act to Regulate Trade between the United States and Countries Practicing State Trading," could be quite simple. It would need to:

(a) Repeal all previous acts bearing on East-West trade;

(b) Provide for control of all phases of U. S. trade with countries in which foreign trade is a monopoly of state agencies;

(c) Grant to the President authority to enter into agreements with the governments of countries affected by the Act and in these agreements to suspend application of controls, including the denial of MFN, in whatever ways and to whatever extent he deemed in the interest of the United States;

(d) Set the following limitations on discretionary authority under the Act (in order to disabuse the communists of any false hopes, and in order to furnish a legislative base for key elements that would be required for the effective use of trade as an instrument of policy in dealing with the communists): (1) exclusion of trade in military and military-related items as defined in the COCOM list; (2) prohibition of private credit to extend beyond regular commercial terms; (3) prohibition of guarantees by government agencies of any credits to extend beyond regular commercial terms or in any event beyond five years; (4) prohibition of negotiations for government-to-government credits; and (5) exclusion from any agreement under the Act of a U. S. commitment to any "barter" deals or arrangements.

Given legislative authority of this type, the Administration could move to the actual negotiation of trade agreements with the particular countries of Eastern Europe, including the USSR, at such times and in such ways and under such circumstances as seemed to it most propitious from the standpoint of furthering U. S. objectives.

What Sort of Trade Agreements?

The U. S. would need for the USSR (and for each of the other East European countries with which it was entering into a new trade relationship) a bilateral arrangement wherein general conditions of trade would be covered in a master agreement and specific details in an annually negotiated "commodities agreement." The general conditions of the master agreement would need to cover exclusions from trade; provisions for the settlement of outstanding claims (for the USSR a Lend-Lease settlement); provisions for mutual protection of copyrights, patent rights, industrial property rights; arrangement for the arbitration of commercial disputes; and arrangements in the form of a government clearinghouse and a licensing system that would enable the two governments (i.e. the U. S.) to keep abreast of performance against provisions of the annual commodity agreement. The commodity agreement would need, in one way or another, to set ceilings on, but not commitments to effect, trade in overall terms and by commodity sectors. For the U. S. this would mean setting import quotas (ceilings) for various Soviet products.

In setting and adjusting these quotas from year to year, the U. S. would have a means to prevent a concentration of categories of goods that traditionally loom largest in Soviet exports, and hence to apply pressure on the Soviets to develop export industries if and when it wanted to make progress in the American market (including, of course, the prevention of dumping).

The master agreement should also cover a variety of matters related directly or indirectly to trade. The U. S. would need to insist upon adjustments in Soviet policies comparable to adjustments that were being effected in U. S. policies. Areas to which the United States would need to particularly direct its efforts would include: the reciprocal establishment of consulates in leading cities of the two countries; the removal of restrictions on diplomatic travel; broadened cultural exchange agreements and practices; greater opportunities for reciprocal exchanges in the area of public information; mutual opening of the two countries at least to publications having to do with or related to trade and commerce; reciprocal opportunities to put on commercial exhibits; mutual access to advertising media for the purpose of promoting trade; improvement in conditions affecting tourism; and so on.

Chapter Forty
REGARDING FOLLOW-UP

The main point in having annually negotiated commodity agreements would be to make possible U. S. changes in the volume and content of trade as broad policy requirements of the United States dictated. This would constitute an essential back-up of a plan to use trade as an "instrument of policy."

If the course of actual commodity exchanges seemed to be working to the advantage of the communists (for example imports were being concentrated almost exclusively on "prototypes"), the United States would be in a position to take remedial action during negotiation of the next annual agreement. And it would be able to do this without any repercussion-producing political fanfare. The U. S. would also be in a position to react if inadequate progress were being made toward the key aim of the United States, that is, the inducement of the communists to develop export industries at a rate roughly comparable to their build-up of imports from the United States; or if the communists were failing to live up to the conditions and general principles provided in the master agreement with regard to the conduct of trade or related matters such as cultural exchanges, etc.; or if political relations deteriorated.

Meanwhile, of course, the fact that the whole trading relationship was within the framework of a continuing and all-encompassing control system would enable the United States to interrupt or otherwise change the course of trade in any way it wished, and at any moment in the case of a political or military crisis. This would give the United States leverage in dealing with the communists that it does not have under the present system, since now there is only a negligible current of trade that could be cut off. The usefulness of this leverage, however, should not be exaggerated. It would more than likely be minimal in itself. But it would constitute an additional weapon in the U. S. arsenal to deal with the favored communist tactic of crisis-mongering. And in cases where the communists were generating a crisis merely for trial balloon purposes or to fish in troubled waters, it might make a difference.

Furthermore, if the U. S. were to develop and try to put into operation a "full grown" plan designed to make trade an immediately important factor in the cold war struggle, it would fail. Trade with the U. S. from the communist standpoint is simply not important enough at present to make it an immediately significant weapon in the cold war struggle, regardless of how the U. S. tries to use it.

What the U. S. will have to do if trade is to become an effective instrument of policy is to firmly fix upon its long-term purposes, and then start to build step by step the capability to achieve those purposes. To accomplish this, it is imperative that the U. S. deliberately proceed to capitalize on its freedom to trade or not to trade as policy considerations demand—without fear that it will thereby do harm to itself.

PART 8

A SUMMARY OVERVIEW OF THE PROBLEM: INCLUDING SOME OPERATIONAL CONCLUSIONS

Chapter Forty-One

A RESTATEMENT OF THE FOURTEEN MOST IMPORTANT POINTS

Of the myriad facts and fancies that intrude themselves into a consideration of the United States East-West trade policy, a few stand out starkly as meriting closest attention and greatest weight. In briefest summary these fourteen are:

— 1 —

The U. S. East-West trade policy is not a policy unto itself. It is one of several interrelated and interdependent policies that make up a strategic design developed over four successive national administrations to cope with the communist threat against the security of the United States and the remainder of the Free World.

A central aim of the design is to deny the communists any fruits from the struggle they wage against the United States, and at the same time to build up the costs of this struggle to the end that the communists will in time abandon it along with the hostility that underlies it.

The policies encompassed in this strategic design range over a wide spectrum; they include among others direct resistance to efforts of communist states to extend their rule by force; developing the capability and will of free peoples to resist communist aggressions from within and without; maintaining U. S. military superiority; demonstrating the superiority of the U. S. economic system; increasing the awareness of vulnerable peoples to the dangers of communist aggression and penetration by either direct or indirect means; countering communist ideological pretensions; denying the communist states equal status or full respectability in the world community of states.

155

The U. S. has spent vast sums, risked global war, and engaged its own forces in local wars in support of these varied policies.

The role of the U. S. trade policy within this strategic design is, on the one hand, to deny the communists the economic and strategic benefits that would come from free access to the U. S. market (and to the extent possible markets of other free countries), and, on the other, to support and further a variety of direct and indirect political ends.

— 2 —

The U. S. trade denial policy is intended to achieve results in conjunction with other policies. It serves to reenforce those other policies and is reenforced by them. It cannot and should not be separated out from other policies and its effectiveness assessed in isolation. It should be treated as an integral part of the overall national strategy.

The possibility exists, however, that world developments have raised new and different strategic requirements for the United States, and that the U. S. strategic design needs to be adjusted accordingly. This possibility has special significance for the trade-policy element in the design. For trade policy, unlike some of the other elements, lends itself to a trial of alternatives within the framework of established strategic objectives.

— 3 —

The communists continue to engage the United States in a struggle in which our national survival is at stake.

The pivotal element in this struggle remains the Soviet Union.

While other communist states, particularly Communist China and Castro's Cuba, pose special dangers to important U. S. interests, the Soviet Union alone has the power to make the struggle global and to threaten the security of the U. S. itself.

Moreover, the policies and activities of the Soviets constitute an essential underpinning for the thrust of the other communist countries, even when coordination is lacking or competition and conflict exists as with Communist China

— 4 —

Significant changes have taken place within the USSR over the past decade. But these have not been in directions that lessen Soviet hostility toward the U. S. or alter the depth of the Soviet commitment to extend, by all feasible means, its system on a world scale. The changes

156

in fact have been largely motivated by the Soviet Union's desire to increase its capability to pursue its objectives against the U. S.

While the Soviet regime shows an awareness of the risks of direct confrontations with the U. S. and concentrates its efforts on indirect methods, including "economic competition between systems," it remains ready to switch to more dangerous forms of struggle when there are promising openings, as for example in the Cuban missile venture.

Moreover, Soviet "competition" with the U. S. in the developing countries has increasingly embroiled the USSR in "wars of liberation" against U. S. positions and interests. These "wars of liberation" and their attendant and related activities now constitute the "motor" of the communist world revolutionary movement and the gravest immediate danger to the United States.

— 5 —

Soviet attitudes, policies, and conduct toward the United States are a product of the Soviet system. More than that, they are in a manner of speaking the essence of the system.

Unless and until the Soviet system itself is changed, and fundamentally so, Soviet hostility toward the U. S. will endure and the Soviet Union will continue to battle as best it can to undermine and destroy the U. S.

— 6 —

An aim of U.S. strategy is to force or induce a change in the Soviet system that would bring an end to Soviet hostility.

A possibility that has been suggested for achieving such a change is the establishment of a new sort of trade relationship between the U. S. and the USSR. A trade policy structured to test whether, in practice, more trade between the communist bloc and the U. S., so the thinking goes, would better serve U. S. strategy—U. S. national purpose— than the present policy of trade denial.

The reasoning here is that extensive trade relations necessarily make for peaceful relations, while the absence of trade makes for hostile relations. Greater trade between the U. S. and the USSR would, it is contended, bring about broadening contacts between Americans and the Soviet people, on both an official and unofficial level, leading to less suspiciousness on the part of the Soviets, increased mutual understanding and respect, and in general a better rapport between the two countries. Greater trade would also, the reasoning goes: create a Soviet stake in more peaceful and tranquil world conditions; involve the Soviets at various levels more deeply in the system that governs free world relationships; produce a U. S. presence in the USSR and make it more of a factor in Soviet political life; and, in broader terms, redirect Soviet competitive urges from aggressive aggrandizements toward peaceful and generally beneficial competition in the trade field.

This line of reasoning does not stand up in the face of hard realities.

Historically, good trade relations have not been synonymous with good political relations. Many of the most intense and enduring political rivalries have been between states which were heavily dependent on each other in the trade field. And some of history's greatest wars have been between close trading partners.

The Soviets, are, moreover, a very special case. Their methods of conducting trade, the whole economic-political system within which trade takes place, carry built-in barriers against trade exercising the kind of influences which are assumed under the "trade as a road to peace" concept.

The Lend-Lease experience of the United States is a glaring example of the failure of even massive trade to affect Soviet attitudes and practices. And Soviet trade relations with all other countries, including members of the communist community itself, have been of the same pattern.

Overall, the matter adds up to this: There seems no realistic prospect that increased trade can be used to bridge the gap of hostility between the U. S. and the USSR or otherwise propel the USSR toward responsible membership in the world community of states.

— 7 —

The Soviet regime views foreign trade as an instrument of struggle, not as a substitute for struggle.

The regime maintains a monopoly over foreign trade activities that enables it to manipulate trade relations at will. Trade is made to serve politics, not the reverse.

And the doctrinal base on which Soviet policy is built holds that capitalist countries, first and foremost of which is the United States, are highly vulnerable to foreign trade maneuverings.

For the long haul, the regime sees the closure of foreign markets as one of the most potent weapons that can be used against the Americans and other "imperialists," since continually expanding foreign markets in its view are essential for the very survival of the capitalist system.

Meanwhile, capitalist hunger for markets can be used by the Soviets to gain immediate advantages in the continuing struggle between systems, advantages that range from obtaining valued assistance from the capitalist countries to build Soviet strength; creating a paralysis-producing dependence on the Soviets among key elements within capitalist "ruling circles"; and generating mounting rivalry, discord, and division within the ranks of the capitalist enemy.

Reversing the coin, the Soviets seek to minimize their own dependence on foreign trade. They buy from advanced countries only as necessary to expand their power base, and sell only as necessary to pay for the limited imports they seek. They concentrate principally on procuring the best machinery, the most advanced industrial plants, equipment embodying the most advanced technology, and the most advanced technical data and know-how.

The Soviet aim is to use the capitalists in order to outstrip the capitalists; to trade in order to eliminate the need for trade.

Any trade in which the Soviets engage is intended to strengthen the Soviet system—either to further an immediate Soviet political objective or to increase the basic capability of the Soviets to achieve success in their "struggle between systems."

— 8 —

Soviet theory and practice regarding foreign trade make certain that the Soviet regime would attempt to turn any efforts the United States might make to establish a new trade relationship between the two countries against the United States. The United States can expect no automatic benefits from a policy that aims at increasing trade.

— 9 —

Economic benefits the U. S. might derive from efforts to improve trade relationships would be minimal, if not negligible.

Soviet theories and practices rule out purchases of U. S. consumer goods or agricultural products except in emergencies.

Moscow would like to buy advanced machinery and equipment on an extensive scale and is evidently all set with an impressive shopping list. But Moscow conditions its broadly conceived purchases program on long-term government-to-government credits.

Lacking credits, Soviet sights admittedly will be drastically lowered. Given free access to the U. S. market, we could expect a flurry of Soviet orders for U. S. items embodying technology not available in Western

Europe and Japan. But evidence indicates the total would probably not exceed $200 million with delivery over several years. There are further indications that orders would taper off sharply once the backlog of urgent technological requirements was met.

Soviet autarkic policies would not alone be responsible; even more important would be the inability of the Soviet Union to pay. With gold reserves at a very low level (under $1.5 billion) and gold shipments continuing to outrun production, and with the Soviet's inability to earn substantial surpluses of hard currencies (Soviet indebtedness to West European countries and Japan is approaching $1 billion, exclusive of mounting long-term debts), the USSR would have to greatly step up sales in the American market to finance any sustained increase in purchases.

U. S. demand for export items available in the USSR (principally crude petroleum, timber, industrial raw materials and low-grade manufactures) is, however, extremely limited; and even if U. S. efforts to expand trade included the granting of Most-Favored-Nation treatment to the Soviets the demand is sure to continue light.

The USSR, with its concentration on heavy industry and otherwise expanding and strengthening its power base, simply lacks the export industries necessary to compete on the American market.

It is possible to calculate an unsubsidized Soviet demand for U. S. goods up to a total $300 million a year by about 1970. The outside limit of Soviet ability to pay, however, will be far under that sum, probably well under $200 million a year as late as 1970. It is in this range, therefore, that we must realistically set our expectations of Soviet purchases from the U. S.—not in the billions talked about by the Soviets and many of our own people.

While this amount would be substantially less than current Soviet purchases in Western Europe, it must be remembered that the U. S. is at a severe disadvantage in competition with the West Europeans, for they are able to absorb far larger volumes of Soviet exports. The only way in which the U. S. can hope to compete successfully with Western Europe in the Soviet market is through granting long-term credits, a step that would amount to subsidizing the Russians since Soviet inability to pay would, in time, catch up with even the longest of long-term credits.

— 10 —

Should the U. S. move to improve trade relations with the USSR and include in its effort the abandonment of its restrictive policies, the USSR would gain substantially in both an economic and political sense.

The regime would be able to satisfy its backlog of demand for advanced U. S. equipment, machinery, complete plants, technical data, and know-how. While the dollar volume involved would be relatively small, current Soviet developmental plans would enjoy a disproportionate boost, since those plans are heavily dependent on the import of just those items of which the U. S. is the leading world producer.

We cannot be sure how great this boost to the Soviets would be, or how much difference it would actually make in their carrying out their plans. A factor to be considered, however, is that in the development of new industries or in increasing the efficiency of old, the margin that spells the difference between progress and floundering can be very thin. During the closing years of the war, for example, the supply of a small number of key items by the U. S. enabled the Soviets to restore, modernize or build from scratch industrial establishments that required an overall investment hundreds of times the value of the U. S. items; yet in most of these cases without the key items from the U. S. nothing could have been done, or great delays and outlandish costs would have had to be incurred.

Another consideration is the tremendous advantage Moscow would derive from the opportunity to pick and choose from among the vast resources available in the American market—both in the way of ongoing production and a unique capability to use advanced technology to create still more advanced technology to meet special needs. *Within the framework of a modest level of trade, the Soviets would be in a position to obtain the best that the United States has to offer to help in the solution of their developmental problems,* as indeed was the case for several trouble-spot industries during the great industrialization drive of the Five Year Plans.

Nor would the benefits stop with the U. S. market alone. The potential offered by the U. S. market could be used as leverage to get better performance and better terms from the West European and Japanese, which in turn could be used as leverage on the Americans. And so on, until the Soviets approached the state postulated by Leninist theory: a state wherein those who are marked for destruction would be scrambling to work for and serve their intended destroyers.

Soviet political gains would be striking and perhaps even more far-reaching than the economic gains.

The U. S. would appear to have been bested in a trial of economic strength with the USSR; the U. S. would have shown itself unable to do without the Russian market; another blow would have been dealt the "position of strength" policy; another demonstration given that the "balance of world forces" had shifted in favor of the USSR. The USSR would be receiving the badge of respectability, the status of full equality in U. S. eyes that it has so long contended was its right.

The change in the U. S. position would signify a weakening of U. S. resolve to hold the line firmly against the USSR, regardless of costs and difficulties. U. S. accommodation to the Soviet regime, without that regime having done anything more than in the past to merit such accommodation, would necessarily undercut the general efforts of the U. S. to marshal the material and moral resources of the free world to protect internal and external frontiers against communist incursions. It would also undercut the U. S. policy of "treating different communist countries differently" according to their conduct, at least insofar as the European communists are concerned.

Soviet confidence in the workings of the "inexorable laws of history that are driving the capitalists to their own destruction" would have been given a great boost; and Soviet claims that history is on the side of their system given added credibility.

— 11 —

The crucial factor in the USSR's current position and prospects is the quiet but deep and many-sided crisis that for some years has been increasingly pressing down on the Soviet regime in both its domestic and external affairs.

The crisis carries with it far-reaching implications for all phases of U. S. policy. It constitutes the essential backdrop and beginning point for judgments and decisions regarding what the U. S. should do about trade.

The crisis has brought the Soviet Union to a crossroads' point in its struggle against the United States, in its drive for world hegemony for its system. The issue at stake for the regime is whether the Soviet Union can long continue to serve its deeply rooted commitments to world communism and its revolutionary goals without bringing disaster on itself.

Among the main elements of the deepening crisis are:

—Shattering of the monolithic character of the world communist movement, with growing conflict and disarray within the communist camp. This has arisen primarily from the deep and lasting break with

162

Communist China but it also involves a decline in Soviet control over the East European satellites.

—Growing commitments and declining returns in the pursuit of international objectives.

—Economic problems and doldrums centering on a slowing growth rate, an increasingly acute resources pinch, a growing crisis in planning and management, a chronic lag in agriculture, inadequate production of consumer items, inability to meet housing requirements, imbalance in meeting planned goals, and falling gold reserves and foreign exchange balances.

—Popular dissatisfaction and restlessness leading to increasing apathy and feet-dragging with respect to demands and exhortations of the regime.

—A loss of momentum, a lack of ability to move toward established domestic and foreign goals.

The crisis is not of a nature to threaten a collapse of the regime or to undermine the basic power of the USSR. Rather it is one of frustration; of the regime's inability to do what it wants to do and is committed to do; of drag, of a slowing down, of not being able to break out of binds and get going again.

— 12 —

The crisis and its varied manifestations have been the major concern of the Soviet leadership over recent years. Measures of all sorts and descriptions have been tried to bring about the solution or elimination of problems. But these measures have been uniformly frustrated by an unwillingness, or inability, of the leaders to touch the Soviet system itself, and it is from the Soviet system that the main elements of the crisis spring.

The leadership therefore is concentrating most of its efforts on effecting a quantum jump of one sort or another that will enable it to bypass or leapfrog the particular problems and difficulties of the moment, and to move to a new power plateau that would serve to generate the momentum needed to move toward the realization of established goals.

The leadership would like to achieve its quantum jump in some easy way; that is by means of a political, or strategic, or technological quick-fix at the expense of the United States. But the policies and alertness of the U. S. is barring the way. Consequently the regime is going it the hard way. It is pouring vast resources and energies into an attempt to achieve an advance in the power sector comparable to the one achieved by Stalin through forced-draft industrialization and collectivization in the thirties, and by the nuclear-rocketry build-up in the fifties.

Concentration is on the attainment of technological preeminence, with space exploration and space science serving as a main lever, but also included are wide-ranging efforts in other fields, such as massive computer utilization, advances in the use of nuclear industry, the development and utilization of new materials, and new methods of control and management.

— 13 —

In the drive for technological preeminence, heavy reliance is being placed on the stepped-up import of the best that the West has to offer in the way of plants, machinery, equipment, technical data and know-how.

In this lies the explanation of the sharp and steady increase (at a rate of over 15 percent per year) in imports from Western Europe and Japan since 1958.

In this also lies the explanation of the great interest of the USSR in the U. S. market. While Moscow may in fact be able to get all that it needs in the way of advanced technology from outside the U. S., it evidently does not think so. *It admittedly wishes to tap the resources and skills of the economically most advanced and powerful of the "capitalist nations." It appears to sense that if it is unable to do this, it will end up frustrated in its hopes for technological supremacy.*

— 14 —

The need of the USSR for outside assistance constitutes a *special vulnerability to U. S. trade policy.* How great this vulnerability is we have no way of knowing. But anxieties of the leadership indicate that it may be of more than passing significance. *The existence of the vulnerability makes it possible for the U. S. to exert influence on the course and outcome of the crisis—through either continuing to deny trade to the USSR or granting access to the U. S. market on a strictly conditional and judiciously controlled basis.*

Chapter Forty-Two

THE OPERATIONAL CONCLUSIONS THAT FOLLOW

— 1 —

From the foregoing points the following broad generalizations necessarily emerge: There is an unbroken continuity in Soviet commitments and aims since the war; these remain as dangerous to the United States to-day as ever; the Soviet regime is finding it increasingly difficult and costly to achieve its aims and carry out its commitments; it nevertheless is persevering in its efforts and is seeking, at mounting costs, to attain technological superiority over the U. S. on the calculation that this will provide a springboard to general superiority, particularly superiority in both economic and strategic power; the regime estimates that because of the "laws that govern capitalism" the U. S. (a) will be unable over the long pull to match the Soviet drive in the technological field, and (b) because of its need for foreign markets can be brought to aid the USSR in achieving the very technological superiority that will contribute so much to U. S. doom.

— 2 —

There is a basic incompatibility between what we know about the methods and purposes of the Soviet regime and the belief that the U. S., through a simple increase in trade can provide the basis for a new and constructive relationship with the USSR.

— 3 —

The United States has no other choice but to accept that any trade policy it has toward the USSR will necessarily be a cold war policy. Whether it is a cold war policy that works in the interest of the United States or one that works in the interest of the Soviet Union will depend on how thoroughly it is grounded in realities.

— 4 —

The United States can serve its national purposes through a continuation of trade denial. It can also, and perhaps better, serve its national purposes through a controlled use of trade to achieve certain specific ends with regard to the USSR and its policies and conduct. It cannot serve its national purposes by simply relaxing and allowing trade to develop as it will.

— 5 —

The possibility that the U. S. can more effectively serve its national purpose through use of controlled trade than through trade denial arises from the deepening crisis in the USSR. The pressing need for outside assistance produced by the crisis makes the Soviets vulnerable to accepting such assistance on a conditional basis. Therefore the U. S. should structure its control system, including the use of import quotas, so as to force the USSR to expand its export industries at a rate roughly corresponding to the increase in its purchases in the U. S. To follow this strategy successfully would require, however, cautious, adroit, and skilled maneuvering on the part of the United States.

— 6 —

The first requirement on the U. S. is to avoid any movement on trade policy, either at its own or Soviet initiative, so long as the communists continue their aggressive war against South Vietnam. The USSR probably has no direct responsibility for this war and probably even fervently wishes it had not happened. Yet the Soviet commitment to the communist world revolutionary cause carries with it an inescapable commitment to the aggression in Vietnam, a fact that Moscow itself openly acknowledges and in accord with which it acts in a variety of ways. Moreover, the Soviet regime is itself embroiled in a "war of liberation" strategy against the U. S., and is under increasingly strong pressure, both external and self-generated, to push forward with that strategy. If the U. S. is to use trade as an "instrument of policy," an essential is that trade operations be adjusted to take account of Soviet acts that are immediately and directly dangerous to U. S. interests. It would seem, therefore, thoroughly inconsistent with this requirement for the U. S. to do other than continue the present restrictive policy until such time as peace is restored in Vietnam, or at least until the Soviets repudiate the struggle raging there.

— 7 —

Another requirement is that the U. S. make haste slowly. A note of urgency is evident in current thinking and planning regarding a change in U. S. trade policy. Actually, no compelling reason exists for any hasty U. S. action. It is, of course, never too early to examine, to explore, to plan, and to prepare. But no compulsions are operating on the U. S. that would require quick movement from preparatory work to decisions and actions.

Hasty action under prevailing circumstances is not only not required but could be quite damaging to U. S. intentions to use trade as a positive instrument of policy. A degree of deliberateness can contribute importantly to the attainment of the greater effectiveness the U. S. seeks in trade relations with the communists, while impatience can lead to premature action that might easily result in the whole business getting out of hand and the loss of an opportunity for the U. S. to replace one system with a better system.

— 8 —

The U. S. should avoid efforts to develop trade for its own sake. The

U. S. has practically nothing to gain from an increase in its Eastern trade as such. The purpose of the United States should be to hold trade down unless and until the Soviets expand their capabilities to supply goods with a ready market in the United States. While the strategy of the United States should be to hold out the *promise* of almost any amount of trade when and as the USSR, through adjustments in its economic system and practices, is in a position to hold up its end of the trade, it should not deliver prematurely on such a promise. Meanwhile, of course, the impact of the promise should not be undercut by individual American businessmen who simply wish to increase trade.

— 9 —

The U. S. should avoid aggressive competition with other industrialized nations of the West. Whatever else the United States may or may not do, it should resist the temptation, which now appears to be approaching an irresistible stage, to grab its allegedly "rightful share" of the Eastern market, through bringing to bear its full competitive power. Tantalizing as may be reports of West European and Japanese export representatives swarming over the hotels and ministries of East European capitals, the U. S. can only lose by entering into aggressive competition with the other industrial countries in the Eastern market. To be successful in such competition, the U. S. would have to engage in a major subsidization operation; and subsidization by the U. S. would impel subsidization by the other western countries, who have far more to lose in the Eastern market than the U. S. has to gain. *The beneficiary would not be the U. S. but the USSR, although individual U. S. enterprises might profit.* Meanwhile, significant harm might be done the already reeling western alliance system.

— 10 —

The U. S. should seek maximum cooperation with the allies. Rather than plunging into a round of wasteful and damaging competition with its allies, the U. S. should continue to strive for a common western policy toward East-West trade. Although unlikely to have significant impact on the military balance of power, *the denial of military and military-related items to the communists from the West is very much to be desired by the United States.* If for no other reason, it is indispensable for the continuation of U. S. support for the military establishment of allied nations. The U. S. will need the continuation of COCOM machinery in order to insure coordination of western policy with regard to items of direct military importance (COCOM list items) and to maintain necessary surveillance.

The U. S. also has a heavy stake in a coordinated western policy with regard to credits and other conditions of trade between the West as a whole and the communists. The agreement of the West Europeans and Japanese to a common policy of limiting credit to what is economically sensible and to otherwise deny the communists an opportunity to derive important advantage from competition among the western states would, of course, make far more effective United States' efforts to use trade to induce a change in production patterns in the USSR and the other communist countries. *Further, the U. S. has as much interest as ever in fostering unbroken alertness throughout the western world to the continuing danger of Soviet communism, and in maintaining the maximum possible unity of purpose and cohesiveness within its alliance system.*

— 11 —

The U. S. will need to extend and refine, not emasculate, its control system. It must be in a position at all times to protect its interests and the interests of its nationals in trade relations with the Soviets and the other East Europeans. It will need controls to enable it to enforce the conditions on the basis of which alone it should be willing to carry on trade—that is, the conditions necessary for the use of trade as an instrument of national policy. In this connection, it will need to have means, including both legislative authority and administrative machinery, to regulate the volume and content of trade as policy demands dictate.

— 12 —

The U. S. will need to operate on a bilateral basis. A natural and necessary extension of a U. S. control system designed to enable a use of trade as a positive instrument of policy would be formal trade agreements between the United States and the USSR and other individual communist countries. This would mark an important departure from the principle of multilateralism on which U. S. trade policies have been based in the past. Such a shift would in many ways be unfortunate. However, the requirements that would flow from an attempt by the U. S. to use trade with the East as a positive instrument of policy could hardly be satisfied otherwise. Beyond this, every other western country that carries on substantial trade with the communists does so on the basis of a bilateral agreement. Any coordinate western policy—which is very much in the U. S. interests to obtain—would make necessary the conduct of U. S. trade also within limits and on conditions spelled out in bilateral agreements.

— 13 —

The U. S. will need to attach certain specific conditions to its trade

168

with the USSR. The Soviets have shown a great interest in a moderation of the U. S. restrictive policy. What they would like most, and will doubtless work diligently for if given any openings, would be a complete abandonment of the policy by the U.S., plus liberal U. S. credit terms, special opportunities in the U. S. market, and other such things that would make for a large-scale trade advantageous to themselves. However, a shift of the U.S. to a policy that would permit increased access to the U. S. market on a measured and controlled basis would still be attractive to the Soviet leaders. The U. S. has every reason to expect, therefore, and should certainly demand, that the USSR meet U. S. movement with movement of its own. The United States cannot use trade to wring important political concessions from the USSR. But it can use it to secure improvements in the Soviet conduct of trade itself, and liberalization of Soviet practices in areas related or relatable to trade. *Aside from a settlement of Lend-Lease claims on a mutually acceptable basis, which would seem a necessary prerequisite for any movement, the U. S. should insist upon arrangements whereby copyrights, patents, and industrial property rights would be protected; treatment of U. S. trade representatives in the USSR in accord with standard norms; consular relations on something of a normal basis; provision for equitable arbitration of commercial disputes; etc.* The U. S. should also insist upon *arrangements that would facilitate more extensive cultural exchanges and an easier flow of ideas across frontiers.* In negotiations with the USSR the U. S. should insist upon the principle that good trade relations require more than a mere exchange of goods; there also must be a freer interflow of information, ideas, and persons.

— 14 —

The U. S. should continue to use trade to promote and support trends toward greater national assertiveness on the part of the Soviet satellites. It would seem to go without saying that the U. S. should be prepared to extend improvements in trade conditions granted the Soviet Union to any of the satellites with which it maintains diplomatic relations. (This condition would exclude East Germany and Albania.) The U. S. would not want, however, to make a broadside extension. It would be to its advantage to negotiate a change in policy with each of the satellites if and as it indicated a desire for such negotiations. In these negotiations, of course, the U. S. could seek, as in the case of the USSR, to secure settlement of bilateral issues relating to trade, and to get a general improvement in conditions governing trade, and the interchanges of information, ideas and persons.

Should circumstances preclude an early shift in U. S. trade policies

*toward the USSR, the U. S. should still stand prepared to move toward
a different trade relationship with any of the satellite countries that demonstrated an interest and a willingness to accept the conditions that
U. S. interests would require. The U. S. should be willing to go a step
further than in the past and use its "differential policy" for inducement
purposes, rather than for mere support of something already underway.*
A beginning might be exploration of the possibility of bilateral agreements within the framework of existing legislation.

— 15 —

*While sticking to a resolve to make haste slowly, the U. S. could still
risk first overtures for a change in trade relationships not only with the
satellites but with the USSR itself.* This might be advantageous to the
United States in that it would enable it to set the framework in which
discussions and negotiations would take place. *The U. S. should, however, put any overtures it makes in low key.* It would be best, initially,
if highly touted trade talks between formal trade delegations were avoided, because of the exaggerated expectations that might be built up, and
because of the likelihood that given such an opening the USSR would
come in with proposals of a nature and magnitude that would get the
whole operation off to a bad start. *The U. S., once it had made first
overture, should be prepared to accept delays and frustrations with calm.
It should, as suggested above, not become too anxious or too much in
a hurry. It should have its aims and goals well in mind before the whole
operation began, and should be prepared to stick to these regardless of
the reaction and the time consumed.*

— 16 —

*U. S. leadership would need to take special care to keep a "new"
U. S. policy in perspective.* A shift in U S. trade policy toward the communists, even if measured, controlled, and directed toward specific policy
ends, will constitute a major turn in the U. S. conduct of cold war
against the communists. The part that the restrictive policy has played
in the overall stance of the United States vis-a-vis the communist danger, the persistence with which the United States has sought to secure
conformance of other nations to the policy, the claims as to the results
that could be expected to flow from it, and a number of other such
circumstances have served to give the policy great symbolic importance.
*This raises the difficult—and quite serious—problem of how to justify
any sort of shift and at the same time safeguard against a general relaxation in the face of the communists. The problem extends into three
dimensions: The American public; the peoples and governments of allied
countries, particularly the peoples; and the peoples and governments of*

the developing countries which are the special targets of communist aggression by indirection.

It would be particularly important that the leadership take the steps necessary to avoid a build-up of expectations that a new trade relationship would serve to bridge the hostility and conflict between the communist and noncommunist worlds; to explain the shift in terms of its usefulness as a means of furthering basic U. S. objectives in the continuing struggle to defeat communist designs; and to minimize the impact of the shift on the continuing efforts of the United States to build unity and cohesiveness within the free world against the communist danger; and to avoid undercutting the long-standing campaign of the U. S. and others to keep authorities in vulnerable countries alert to the dangers of communist infiltration and subversion through economic and other means.

THE NATIONAL ASSOCIATION OF MANUFACTURERS, formed in 1895, is a voluntary organization which serves as the national and international spokesman for American industry. The membership is made up of every type and size of company and accounts for approximately 75 percent of the U.S. manufacturing output. Working basically through committees which deal with a wide range of problems, the Association fosters sound programs for advancement of the economic well-being and social progress of the American people.

The International Economic Affairs Committee, under whose auspices this monograph is published, is responsible for formulation of basic NAM policies and for taking action, by all appropriate means, to:

> Promote expanded world trade and investment.

> Expand and secure private enterprise institutions—both economic and political—throughout the world.

> Protect the property rights—tangible, intangible and intellectual —of United States companies operating abroad.

> Cooperate with, influence and assume responsibility for decision-molding in significant international organizations.

The Committee's policy recommendations in the international area become, upon adoption by the Board of Directors, official positions of the Association.

Other Publications of the NAM on Current International Economic Affairs

BLU-TRADE

An Opportunity for Business and Government Leaders at State and Local Levels to Show the Way to Patriotic Profit Through Export

DIRECT INVESTMENT ABROAD AND THE U.S. BALANCE OF PAYMENTS

An address by Richard C. Fenton, President, Pfizer International

WEBB-POMERENE ASSOCIATIONS

Date of Operation, Method of Operation, Products Exported and Statistical Analysis of Activity (1963)

CREATIVE FERMENT IN WORLD PATENT SYSTEMS

Conference Papers From World Patent Conference, June 1965, New York City, under auspices of NAM Patents Committee

Miscellaneous papers on monetary, economic, trade and related problems may be obtained upon request to the International Affairs Division, NAM.

DATE DUE

OC 3 '69			
OC 1 7 '69			
NO 5 '69			
NO 1 9 '69			
GAYLORD			PRINTED IN U.S.A.